OTHER VOLUMES

TO BE PUBLISHED ARE:

Nature

Freedom

The Human Face

Man at Work

Death

Charity

The Experience of God

The Family

Festivals

ALREADY IN PRINT:

War and Peace

Music

Man and Animal

Education

Man
through
his Art

VOLUME **5**

LOVE AND
MARRIAGE

The general concept of the series has the approval of UNESCO, but the detailed selection of material for inclusion in each volume has been the responsibility of the authors, endorsed by the World Confederation of Organizations of the Teaching Profession (WCOTP).

New York

Graphic   *Greenwich, Connecticut*

Society Ltd.

FIRST EDITION 1968

Library of Congress number 68-11207

Published by E. P. Publishing Company Limited for
EDUCATIONAL PRODUCTIONS LIMITED, 17 Denbigh Street, London SW1

Printed in Italy
7158   0324   7

4

General preface

LOVE AND MARRIAGE are intensely personal experiences. The Editors, who assembled the examples of art and prepared the accompanying commentaries for this fifth volume in the series 'Man through his Art,' must have sensed that they were dealing with a fabric whose delicacy almost precludes examination without defacement. The Editors have here continued their exploration of the varied aspects of human life and have placed before the reader a wide range of examples which show how various cultures have given artistic expression to them.

Although the art forms the Editors have selected do not in themselves explain the differing cultural relationships, customs, and value judgements, they do help to show how love and marriage have been perceived in different cultures and at different epochs.

William G. Carr, Secretary-General,
World Confederation of Organizations of the Teaching Profession

Editors and contributors

EDITORS   **Madame Anil de Silva.**

Professor Otto von Simson.

Philip Troutman.

ASSOCIATE EDITORS   **Sēnake Bandaranayake,**
Queen's College, Oxford.

Professor Soichi Tominaga,
Director of the National Museum of Western Art,
Tokyo, Japan.

EDITORIAL ASSISTANT   **Alix Comte**

CONTRIBUTORS   **Sēnake Bandaranayake,**
Queen's College, Oxford.

Marcel Brion,
Académie Française.

Professor François Chamoux,
Department of Greek and Roman Antiquities,
The Sorbonne, Paris.

Alexander Eliot,
author of *American Painting*, etc.

Mrs. H. A. Groenewegen-Frankfort,
author of *Arrest and Movement in Art*, etc.

Dr. John Hayes,
The London Museum, Kensington Palace, London.

Professor Hans Kauffmann,
Professor Emeritus, Die Freie Universität, Berlin,
author of *Donatello*, etc.

R. H. Pinder-Wilson,
Department of Oriental Antiquities, The British
Museum, London.

Professor Jakob Rosenberg,
National Gallery of Art, Washington,
author of *Rembrandt*, etc.

Madame Anil de Silva,
author of *The Life of Buddha* and *Chinese Landscape
Painting from the Caves of Tun-Huang*.

Professor Otto von Simson,
Die Freie Universität, Berlin,
author of *The Gothic Cathedral*, etc.

William B. Trousdale,
Freer Gallery of Art, Washington.

Jean-Louis Vaudoyer,
Académie Française,
author of *Paul Cézanne*, etc.

6

Contents

Acknowledgements

THE EDITORS cannot record their thanks individually to all those who have given their disinterested help and encouragement to this project from its inception.

Special thanks are due to the Asia Society, New York, who provided assistance for the preparative work of this project; to the Unesco Secretariat, without whose constant guidance and active assistance this project could not have materialized.

A debt of appreciation is also acknowledged to the National Commissions for Unesco of Cambodia, the Federal Republic of Germany, France, Great Britain, India, Italy, New Zealand, the Sudan, Sweden, the UAR, and the USA. The illustrations are reproduced by the courtesy of the following museums, private collectors and photographers.

Introduction Fig. a, Tutankhamen Collection, Cairo Museum: photo Hirmer Verlag, Munich; Fig. b, British Museum, London; Fig. c, photo Musée Guimet, Paris; Fig. d, photo A. Martin, Paris; Fig. e, photo Real-photo, Paris; Fig. f, photo Jean Dominique Lajoux, Paris; Fig. g, Rijksmuseum, Amsterdam; Fig. h, Mellon Coll., National Gallery of Art, Washington, D.C.; Fig. i, Kunsthistorisches Museum, Vienna; Fig. j, Nolde-Museum, Seebüll; Fig. k, photo Marc Vaux, Paris.
Plate 1, Cairo Museum: photo Hirmer Verlag, Munich. Fig. 1a, Cairo Museum: photo Vigneau, Paris; Fig. 1b, Rijksmuseum van Oudheden, Leiden. Plate 2, Museo Civico, Palermo: photo Alinari. Fig. 2a, The Metropolitan Museum of Art, New York; Walter C. Baker Fund, 1956. Plate 3, Vatican Museum, Rome: photo Scala, Florence. Fig. 3a, Museo Profano, Vatican: photo Alinari, Florence; Fig. 3b, Museo Nazionale di Villa Giulia, Rome: photo Alinari, Florence; Fig. 3c, Museo Nazionale, Naples: photo Mansell Collection, London; Fig. 3d, Villa di Papa Giulio, Rome: photo Anderson-Giraudon, Rome-Paris; Fig. 3e, Photo Alinari, Rome. Plate 4, photo Werner Bischof-Magnum Photos, Paris. Fig. 4a, photo Ecole Française d'Extrême Orient, Hanoi, Archives Musée Guimet, Paris; Fig. 4b, photo Henri Cartier-Bresson, Magnum Photos Inc., Paris; Fig. 4c, photo A. Martin, Paris; Fig. 4d, photo Archaeological Survey of India, Govt. of India, New Delhi. Plate 5, Formerly National Museum, Peking. Figs. 5a and 5b, Collection Marcel Brion, Paris: photo Alix Comte, Paris. Plate 6 and Fig. 6a, Staatliche Museen, Berlin-Dahlem: photo Walter Steinkopf, Berlin. Plate 7, Collection and photo Bibliothèque Nationale, Paris. Fig. 7a, Bibliothèque Nationale, Paris: photo Babey, Basle. Plate 8, National Gallery, London: photo John R. Freeman, London. Fig. 8a, National Gallery, London. Plate 9, Collection and photo The Cleveland Museum of Art, E. and L. E. Holden Funds, Cleveland, Ohio; Fig. 9a, Cleveland Museum of Art, Cleveland, U.S.A.; Fig. 9b, Gotha Museum: photo Bildarchiv, Marburg; Fig. 9c, Musée de Cluny, Paris: photo Bulloz, Paris. Plate 10, Collection and photo Österreichische Nationalbibliothek, Vienna. Fig. 10a, Bibliothèque Nationale, Paris; Fig. 10b, photo Instituto Geografico de Agostina Novara – C. Berilacona; Fig. 10c, The Minnesinger Ms. Universitätsbibliothek, Heidelberg. Plate 11, British Museum, London: photo John R. Freeman, London. Fig. 11a, India Office Library, London; Fig. 11b, India Office Library: Photo R. B. Fleming, Ltd., London. Plate 12, Alte Pinakothek, Munich: photo Blauel. Figs. 12a and 12b, Bibliothèque Nationale, Paris; Fig. 12c, National Gallery, London. Plate 13, Collection and photo Rijksmuseum, Amsterdam: Text by courtesy of Phaidon Press, London. Figs. 13a and 13b, Metropolitan Museum of Art, New York; Benjamin Altman bequest, 1913. Fig. 14a, Victoria and Albert Museum, London; Fig. 14b, Kasturbhai Lallbhai Collection, India; Fig. 14c, Victoria and Albert Museum, London. Fig. 15a, Universitätsbibliothek, Heidelberg; Fig. 15b, National Museum, New Delhi: photo Bulloz, Paris; Fig. 15c, National Museum, New Delhi; Fig. 15d, Cleveland Museum of Art, Cleveland, U.S.A. – George P. Bickford collection. Plate 16, National Gallery, London: photo John R. Freeman, London. Fig. 16a, National Gallery, London. Plate 17, British Museum, London: photo John R. Freeman, London. Fig. 17a, Musée Guimet, Paris; Fig. 17b, Photo Giraudon, Paris. Plate 18, Collection Rockefeller Institute of Medical Research, New York: photo Dessin Cadres. Fig. 18a, Louvre Museum, Paris; photo Giraudon, Paris. Plate 19, Collection and photo Musée des Beaux-Arts, Tournai – Admin. Communal de Tournai, Service de Tourisme et des Beaux-Arts, Tournai. Fig. 19a, Musée des Beaux-Arts, Tournai: photo Jules Messiaen, Tournai; Fig. 19b, Courtauld Institute, London. Plate 20A, photo Henry Moore. Plate 20, collection and photo Art Institute, Chicago. Fig. 20a, Craiova Museum of Art, Rumania; Fig. 20b, Collection of the artist: photo Marc Vaux, Paris.

Introduction

THIS book begins with a serene and formal painted sculpture of an Egyptian Pharaoh and his wife; it ends with emotion-charged forms of the contemporary sculptors Moore, Zadkine and Brancusi, *King and Queen*, *The Couple*, and *The Kiss*. For the artist, as for the poet and philosopher, the relationship of man and woman – sensual and spiritual, social and economic, romantic, practical and ideal – has provided a theme of eternal fascination and human interest.

Each of the works of art reproduced in this book illuminates an aspect of this relationship in the style and from the viewpoint of a particular time and place. In this sense LOVE AND MARRIAGE is a kind of social history or gallery of the institution of marriage and the attendant rituals and attitudes which man has created around it. But marriage is only a legal or ritualistic framework for human love, and love will not be impersonalized. No other subject in the world's great art speaks to us more immediately and directly, however remote the setting in time or place. The Egyptian Pharaoh and his queen depicted on the Tutankhamen chest cover are young lovers, even today as emotionally evocative to us in their way as the arresting *Slovenes* painted by the modern German artist Nolde, illustrated at the end of this introduction.

From the sensual basis of the love between male and female, man has developed profound and beautiful symbolisms. This is particularly true in Indian art. The Indian mind has made no distinction between the sacred and the profane. In the Indian experience, love between man and woman is the realization of an all-embracing cosmic principle, male and female appearing as complementary aspects of the absolute reality. In the myth of the god Shiva and his goddess Parvati, the god embodies virility, power and valor; his goddess the feminine principle. Neither can exist without the other. In India marriage is understood to be a re-enactment of this myth. On the day of the marriage, the bridal couple are raised to the dignity of god and goddess, worshipped by their parents and relatives with the ritual offering of lights and

Fig. a. *Tutankhamen and his wife. Egypt. XVIIIth Dynasty.*

Fig. b. *Ashur-bani-pal feasting with his Queen in the royal garden. Assyria.* 660 BC.

Fig. c. *'La Correction Maritale'. Medieval wood-carving, the church of Brou, Bourg, France.*

Fig. d. *Husband and wife. Medieval funerary stele, France.*

flowers which is made to a god in his temple. The Indian epics are full of expressions of the depth of feeling of the love thus deified. In the *Ramayana of Valmiki*, Sita says to Rama when he is exiled to the forest:

'A wife shares her husband's life. For a woman there is no other destiny but that of her husband. When you go into the forest, O Bull among men, I will go before you and clear your path . . . it is sweeter to follow a husband than to live in a rich palace. Even Heaven without you would be odious to me . . . A thousand seasons will be as one sweet day. All will be joy . . . I shall fear neither fatigue nor distress . . . I will not grieve for my home, for anywhere without you, my Rama, is as hell . . . I have no other refuge but you.'

Western thought has also transfigured human love. The poetic fervor of the *Song of Solomon* is a part of the Old Testament:

'The voice of my beloved! behold, he cometh,
Leaping upon the mountains, skipping upon the hills.
My beloved is like a roe or a young hart:

Fig. e. *The Suitor's Visit. Gerard Ter Borch. Holland. 1617–1681.*

Fig. f. *Clockwork Gondola. South Germany. 16th Century.*

Behold, he standeth behind our wall,
He looketh in at the windows,
He showeth himself through the lattice.
My beloved spoke, and said unto me,
"Rise up, my love, my fair one, and come away.
For, lo, the winter is past,
The rain is over and gone;
The flowers appear on the earth;
The time of the singing of birds is come,
And the voice of the turtle is heard in our land;
The fig tree ripeneth her green figs,
And the vines are in blossom,
They give forth their fragrance.
Arise, my love, my fair one, and come away.
O my dove, that art in the clefts of the rock, in the
        covert of the steep place,
Let me see thy countenance, let me hear thy voice;
For sweet is thy voice, and thy countenance is comely."'

The Song of Songs

Fig. g. *Prince William II and Mary Stuart. Anthony van Dyck. Flanders (mod. Belgium). 1641.*

Fig. h. *The Brothers Van Gogh. Ossip Zadkine. 1964.*

The ascetic mind of the medieval Christian church saw this poem as an allegory of the love of God and the Church, for love has been conceived in the western as well as in the eastern tradition as a mystery which leads upward to the perception of ultimate truth, either in a philosophic sense, or as the union of man and God – which in nearly all world religions is experienced as love.

But marriage is a more practical condition. For every social group, the establishment of a firm structure for the preservation of the family and the perpetuation of property has been of the first importance. The dignity of the marriage rite has been deliberately enhanced by myth and symbolism, in poetry, in legend, and in art, as in such works as the solemnly beautiful *Marriage of Zeus and Hera* from the Temple of Selinunte.

At the same time, the business nature of the marriage contract has been frankly recognized in most periods, sometimes to such a point that the wife herself became simply another piece of property. The Greek writer Xenophon is quoted in Madame Lilar's book *Aspects of Love*. The young bridegroom Ischomachos meets Socrates in the market place, and within this excerpt he relates to him a conversation with his wife:

Fig. i. *A Couple. Badami, India. 6th Century* AD.

'Ischomachos is proud of having himself educated his young wife, at the end of which education he had only to speak a word to be obeyed at once. Complacently he recounts his first conversation with her after marriage. "When she was used to me and was tame enough for a talk, I asked her these questions, more or less: Tell me, my wife, do you understand for what purpose I have married you and for what purpose your parents gave you to me? Neither you nor I was at a loss to find someone to sleep with: you know this, I am sure, as well as I. But after both I on my behalf and your parents on yours had given much thought to the best associate we could take to us for our house and our children, I for my part chose you, and your parents, it seems to me, chose me, from among the possible partners." And when his wife (who was fifteen) asked in agitation: "What can I do? All depends on you. My mother has told me my business is to be good." Ischomachos replied: "The duty of a good man and his wife is to keep their property in the best possible state and to increase it as much as possible by honorable and lawful means." This tells us where we are: What Ischomachos taught was merely the art of getting rich.'

When such economic attitudes toward marriage became too oppressive, the human imagination was apt to burst forth in extravagant fictions and idealizations of illicit love, such as the medieval codes of courtly love or the Oriental and Arabic romances, which have been so charmingly illustrated in miniatures and manuscript illuminations.

Whatever the view of romantic love or the economics of marriage arrangements, the works of art depicting betrothal and marriage do tell of an essential human experience: the unity and common outlook of a man and a woman living in partnership, sharing the same concerns

13

Fig. j. *Rama and Sita. Prambanon, Java. 9th Century* AD.

and destiny. Again and again in these works, two figures stand, hands joined, facing their world. This is the social and permanent reality of marriage.

With it, there is another reality of individual feeling, as universal as property and partnership, as present in these works of art as it is in the words of the poets of every era.

'The pain of loving you
Is almost more than I can bear.
I walk in fear of you.
The darkness starts up where
You stand, and the night comes through
Your eyes when you look at me.
Ah never before did I see
The shadows that live in the sun . . .'

A Young Wife,   D. H. Lawrence.

'In the heavens we shall be twin birds in flight,
On earth we shall be two trees whose branches entwine.'

Chinese, 8th Century A.D.

C. Edgar Phreaner

Bibliography

Mme. Lilar
Aspects of Love
Thames and Hudson, London, 1964

John Smith
Modern Love Poems
Studio Vista, London, 1966

1 Rahotep and Nofret

Painted Limestone sculpture, from Egypt. Fourth Dynasty, 2723–2563 BC

IMAGES OF HUSBAND AND WIFE occur quite frequently together in Egyptian art, both in statuary and, rather later, in reliefs and paintings, but the portrayal is remarkably reticent about their conjugal relationships. In statuary the figures are either simply juxtaposed or linked in a purely formal manner: the woman's arm is laid round her husband's waist or shoulder. If this was intended to denote affection it lacked erotic overtones, for the same lifeless disposition of arms – which barely deserves the term gesture – may indicate a parental relationship or one between a goddess and the king, while, significantly, there is no record of a husband embracing his wife, except in one revolutionary period. In fact the chastity of Egyptian art – one might call it emotional frigidity – is practically unrelieved.

To see this curious fact in the right perspective it is not sufficient to point out that most Egyptian art had a tomb as its setting, for the lack of funereal solemnity in the scenes of daily life covering the tomb walls is too well known for comment. The question remains, what concepts of the Hereafter found expression in such complex funeral practices. It is undeniable that these were rooted in very primitive magic rites and a naïve preoccupation with the possible needs of the dead. But it is equally clear that the art which 'flowered unseen' in the tombs was prompted by a deep and reverent love of life, which transcended the greed and the fear of magic wish fulfilment. This love of life embraced the most varied aspects of worldly existence and fostered a desire for the interpenetration of the two realms, the Here and the Beyond. Through the provision of a tomb, a House of Eternity as it was called, death became ever present in life, for it made constant demands on the living. Inside the tomb, however, the typical and recurrent features of all those activities which sustain and enrich life were 'eternalised' in the form of lively scenes. These, though they often had a bearing on food production, ranged widely over man's activities and were to be a lasting presence for the dead. A similar approximation of life and death also informed the earliest, and through Egyptian history the most imposing, statues of the tomb-owners, who were portrayed as both alive and lifeless – lifeless in the sense that their bodies, inexorably caught in a harsh cubic framework, appear to be less in repose than incapable of movement. Even the stance with one leg forward, which in standing figures was copied from the reliefs, hardly ever suggests a stride or even a potential movement. The often highly individualized faces, on the other hand, can be staggeringly lifelike, with inlaid eyeballs and crystal pupils of mysterious depths. Generally speaking, the bodies of such statues, in their frozen immobility, are a denial of ephemeral life, while the faces appear to defy death. In conjunction they embody the paradox – so often glibly used – of 'life everlasting'.

It is in perfect accord with Egyptian concepts that the keynote of their entombed images should be one of complete serenity. Even when depicted as man and wife the figures are entirely self-contained, and though a child may be added to form a family group, there is a marked lack of emphasis on motherhood with its emotional implications. If this resulted in a rather bald statement of the fact of matrimony, as a statement it has remarkable implications: apparently the

Generalizations on Egyptian art often prove to be false. Nevertheless, indulging in them is justified. For, when confronted with Egyptian works of art, the uninitiated may find himself torn between two conflicting experiences; a sense of familiarity, of human proximity on the one hand, and on the other a sense of being face to face with a totally alien world. It seemed, therefore, appropriate to bring into focus the metaphysical paradox which lies at the root of all the more important Egyptian monuments. It is, however, undeniable that what we have called 'the interpenetration of the temporal and the timeless' was not formally settled once and for all in the Old Kingdom, when so many canons of representation were fixed for the first time. The history of Egyptian art shows that at some times a deepening of religious concepts was expressed in slightly altered forms, and at other times we notice a departure either in the direction of a strict formal rigidity or in the opposite direction towards a trivial naturalism. The latter, in particular, the familiarity of which will delight the casual observer, appears to contradict our attempt to interpret the character of Egyptian art in general terms. But the contradiction is more apparent than real. It is very striking that whenever a period of great achievement follows one

Fig. 1a. *Rahotep and Nofret.*

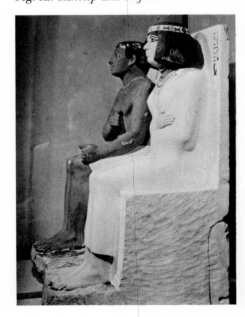

Stone Sculpture, ca. 2723–2563 B.C.
Approximately 48 in. : 122 cm.

1. RAHOTEP AND NOFRET
Cairo Museum

Fig. 1b. *Maya and Merit. Egypt. XVIIIth Dynasty.*

of formal, as well as political disintegration, the emphasis is again on what we have called the religious paradox of 'life everlasting'. This paradox, though it informs nearly all funeral art, has been expressed most superbly in the portrayal of the divine king.

H.A.G.-F.

Bibliography

Lange and Hirmer
Egypt
Phaidon Press, London, 1956

H. A. Groenewegen-Frankfort
Arrest and Movement in Art
Faber and Faber, London, 1951

Christiane Desroches-Noblecourt
Tutankhamen
New York Graphic Society, Greenwich, Connecticut. 1963

Christiane Desroches-Noblecourt
Ancient Egypt: The New Kingdom and the Amarna Period. New York Graphic Society, Greenwich, Connecticut. 1961

bond between husband and wife was considered important enough to be 'eternalised'. Moreover, the earliest couple known to us, Rahotep and Nofret, are represented as of equal stature. Since this became a fairly general rule, both in free-standing groups and in tomb reliefs when the owner and his wife are shown 'watching' scenes of daily life, we may assume that married women were highly regarded even in the absence of textual evidence on their legal or social status.

Equally significant in our Plate is the artist's subtle characterisation of Nofret's passive, slightly secretive femininity by the side of her energetic, openfaced husband. The very awareness of the contrast suggests a by no means primitive relationship between the sexes. However, the all-pervading desire for a timeless existence after death deprived Egyptian funeral art of emotional expressiveness, which by its very nature is timebound.

Although this holds good for most of Egypt's millennial history, and although minor attempts – usually in decadent periods – at relaxing the very strict stylistic code rarely produced great works of art, a deliberate subversion of traditional values took place in the reign of the heretic king Akhenaten. His monotheistic sun-worship has by now become common knowledge, less so its implications. Under his influence there occurred a resolute turning away from the night-side of existence, the preoccupation with 'life everlasting'. Actuality, life in time and space, non-typical dramatic and emotional situations became a major concern in scenic art. And since interest was mainly focussed on the king and his family, the living centre of the newly founded community at el Amarna, the king was no longer represented in the rigidly hieratic poses, which the dogma of divine kingship had demanded throughout. On the contrary, great emphasis was laid on his ephemeral acts and the intimacy of his family life. We see the royal couple, lovingly entwined, riding in their chariot, embracing their children, even enjoying a meal together. It is not surprising that Amarna artists, inspired as well as baffled by the new emphasis on sentiment, were rarely successful in depicting the raptures of the royal family, and often produced caricatures. It is even more disappointing that we cannot judge whether this sentimental image of family life was a projection of commonly shared ideals, for it was never applied to the king's subjects. The new style, which ran counter to values accepted for so long, so unquestioningly, was nearly as short-lived as the heresy which brought it into being. Nearly, but not quite. The tenderness of marital love, often so clumsily portrayed in Amarna, found expression once again after the collapse of the Amarna revolt, not in a tomb relief or painting, where it would have been incongruous, but on an object of secular use (Introduction, Fig. a). Akhenaten's successor, the youthful Tutankhamen, and his queen are portrayed on an ivory chest. The two young people appear as frail as the flowers offered by the bride and acknowledged by the bridegroom with the same gesture of adoration as kings reserved for the godhead. It is the 'immortal' confrontation of young lovers, revealed at a moment in time. As such it was also the final flowering of Akhenaten's bid – doomed to fail – for liberation from a tyrannical faith in the transcendent value of a timeless Hereafter.

Nevertheless, when shortly after the Amarna period man and wife are again portrayed in traditional funerary statues, we find a subtle change. In Fig. 1b Maya and Merit have a worldly elegance, a distinction, which alters the character of their other-worldly immobility. These beautiful creatures appear united by a personal bond too deep for an explicit gesture. They remind one of a devoted regal couple presiding over a solemn festival. They lack the naïvety of an earlier religious faith; their serenity hovers on the brink of secularity, a stage never reached, for better or for worse, in Egyptian funerary art.

H. A. Groenewegen-Frankfort

2 The Marriage of Zeus and Hera

Marble relief from the Greek temple at Selinus, Sicily. c. 480–470 BC

IN THIS SIMPLE COMPOSITION we see Zeus, the god of the Sky and the most powerful of the Greek gods, sitting on a rock. He leans back on his left hand. With his right he holds the wrist of his wife Hera and draws her towards him. Hera stands before him enveloped in her veil. She wears a long linen tunic, over which she has draped obliquely a sort of scarf of fine wool. This was the costume worn by the women of Ionia, the eastern region of Greece. Over this dress the goddess wears a woollen veil with large pleats, which passes over her head and shoulders down to the floor. This is a special feature of the costume worn by the brides of that time. The bride wrapped herself in the veil on her wedding day and hid her face under it until the moment when she unveiled herself before her husband. This was, very often, the first time they saw each other. This is precisely what Hera is doing before her husband Zeus on this metope from Temple E at Selinus (see note). She draws her veil aside to show herself to him and he takes possession of his young wife by taking her wrist. The sculptor has represented the divine pair as a young married couple in Greece in the fifth century BC.

We have here a manifestation of the well-known tendency in Greek art and religion to represent the gods as human beings, living a similar life and expressing the same feelings as men do in earthly society; it is what we call anthropomorphism.

Though the gods were transposed into an ideal world and were immortal, their life was very similar to that of the people who worshipped them. They were represented as the most beautiful and the most powerful of men, who did not fall under the natural law of life and death. With these exceptions they were just as susceptible to the passions, the joys and even the suffering of ordinary mortals. We see in our plate the very profound and yet very basic feeling of attraction that exists between man and woman. The god, in whose powerfully modelled torso the sculptor has embodied the dominant male force, draws his companion towards him with an unmistakable authority. There is no force or brutality in his action, and at the same time as he manifests his sovereign will the god is so clearly captivated by the radiant beauty of his divine wife, who stands unveiled before him.

Greek artists have captured these sentiments in a few expressive works. We have some funerary steles of the fifth and fourth centuries BC, which present, side by side, a husband and wife separated by death. Often they exchange a tender greeting or hold hands as a symbol of their mutual affection. Some vase-paintings represent the ceremony of preparation before a marriage procession or the marriage procession itself (see Fig. 2a). But no work of Greek art expresses better the force of feeling and emotion between a man and a woman, and the ties of marriage, than this justly celebrated relief of the divine couple, Zeus and Hera. The god submits to the law of nature, that great law which incites union and transmits and perpetuates life. There is a great deal of solemnity on this occasion where the creative urge of the man meets the confident expectation of the woman, so sure of herself; the marriage unites the force of the one and the beauty of the other. It is no less than a symbol of marriage which is represented here, a celebration of marriage as one of the great

The temple from which this sculpture was taken, was a shrine consecrated to the goddess Hera. Perhaps the sculptor was inspired by the famous passage from the *Iliad*, which describes the meeting of Zeus and Hera on Mount Gagaros. Zeus, at the sight of his wife, feels transported with love and desire and draws her to him behind a cloud, to be concealed from indiscreet eyes.

The Greeks of Selinus who looked at this *metope* above the colonnade of their temple must have been reminded of that part of their religious rites where, at certain festivals, the priest and his wife had to perform the sacred union of the god and his divine spouse (a practice known as *hierogamy*). This ritual was meant to remind the people of the immortal favour which guaranteed their fecundity. It is appropriate that this image, which an unknown classical artist has created, evokes with such expressive force the elementary sentiment of the mutual attraction of a man and a woman, conscious that they hold in the secret of their union the future of humanity.

F.C.

Fig. 2a *A Marriage Procession. Attic Vase by the Amasis Painter. Greece. ca. 560 BC.*

2. THE MARRIAGE OF ZEUS AND HERA
Museo Civico, Palermo

Marble relief, *ca.* 480-470 BC.

The 'metope' is an ornamental feature in Greek architecture, a stone plaque which was placed between two decorative elements called *triglyphs* or blocks of stone decorated with vertical crenellations; the *metopes* and *triglyphs* together formed a frieze which was placed above a colonnade or at the top of a wall in a Doric temple. The *metopes* might be decorated with sculptured reliefs, as in the case of the Doric temple at Selinus in Sicily. This particular temple at Selinus is known as *Temple E*, because it is one of the ruined temples at Selinus which have not been identified.

Temple E was constructed about 480–470 BC. The sculptures are in the pre-classic or *severe style*, a period just before that of the Parthenon in Athens and the work of the Great sculptor Phidias. This style is characterised by a great simplicity and nobility, which still has a trace of archaism in the treatment of the faces and the hair. It is called the *severe style* because of the gravity of the faces, which never smile.

The *metopes* of Temple E are carved in limestone, heavily eroded by long exposure. But the faces, the bare arms and feet of the female figures are carved in marble which had been attached to the limestone relief, as in the figure of Hera in our plate. Being a much harder material, the marble is less decayed than the limestone.

The joins between the marble and the limestone and the differences in colouring were not at first noticeable, since the sculptures and reliefs, in their original state, were painted over in the most vivid colours. It takes a great effort of imagination today to visualize the original appearance of Greek sculpture in its bright colours, which have now almost entirely disappeared. The decorative effect of the sculptural detail in Greek architecture was emphasized by these colour effects (mostly in blues and reds, but with some yellow, green and violet). Details of anatomy and drapery were more easily distinguishable at a distance because of the variations in colour. (There were also ornaments in metal, usually bronze, which was allowed to remain in its naturally gilded state.) Greek sculpture, in losing its polychrome finish, has probably lost a great deal of the dramatic effect it must have had on the ancient Greeks. The *metopes* of Temple E still retain faint traces of their original colouring.

F.C.

Bibliography

François Chamoux
Greek Art
Pallas Library of Art
New York Graphic Society, Greenwich, Connecticut. 1966

institutions of the human and the divine order.

Marriage had a particular significance in the social structure of Greek society. The social unit in which the Greeks lived was the city, a small group of a thousand or even of a few hundred men, confined (with rare exceptions) to a limited territory. The citizens of this social group possessed their civic status by right of birth. A citizen had to be born of a free father and not of a stranger nor of a slave. The birth had to take place within a legal union, so that it would not be the object of any dispute. Children born of a concubine could not be considered citizens, except under certain conditions. Only legitimate children, solemnly recognized by their father, could be admitted, with full rights, into the civic body. One understands, then, the especial importance of marriage, for it guaranteed the continuity of the city and the legal purity of the civic body. This was the reason why the institution of marriage was treated with such great respect in Greek civilisation. Hera, an important goddess of the Greek pantheon and the wife of the supreme God Zeus, had a special role as the protectress of marriage. Strict rules rigorously protected marriage from anything which might harm the legitimacy of the children; a wife's adultery was punished very severely and seducers were given very heavy sentences; a husband who caught his wife in adultery was entitled to kill the guilty lovers.

The social character of marriage was more important to the Greeks than the emotions and sentiments it involved. Generally, a husband and wife scarcely knew each other before the marriage. For both the young man and for the girl, the decision was taken by their parents. It was above all an alliance useful to the two families concerned. The personal feelings of the future partners played no part in the decision. The love and affection there might be between a husband and wife would have to develop after the marriage. This was certainly true of the Archaic and Classical periods, up to about the end of the fourth century BC. From about this period onwards there seems to have been a change of attitude – for instance, the comedies of the Greek poet Menander (who lived at the end of the fourth century BC) often have as their theme the story of a young man and woman in love, who are separated by circumstances until finally more favourable circumstances enable them to get married. Before this period, however, love played no part in the marriage celebration which was a unique and all-important social ceremony.

Naturally this does not mean that the Greeks did not know conjugal love, but it was essentially something which arose and developed after marriage. While the husband (for whom the home was, as it were, the centre from which he operated) was away from his home, engaged in his work or in the affairs of the city, the wife reigned over the slaves and the children and managed the domestic economy. She was in every sense the mistress of the house and her husband respected her in this capacity. They shared, to some extent, a common life and at the same time they had between them a careful division of their respective spheres of activity, thereby achieving a balanced and durable relationship.

Certainly Greek social customs did not prevent a man from having relationships outside marriage, with courtesans or slaves. Public opinion was very indulgent towards such distractions, which were considered normal for a man. But if such relations throw some light on certain forms of sensual pleasure indulged in by the Greeks they have little to do with the essentially conjugal passion such as existed (say) between Penelope and Ulysses in the *Odyssey* or Hector and Andromache in the *Iliad*. Marriage and the family were unique institutions for which the Greeks always had a profound respect.

François Chamoux

3 The Aldobrandini Marriage

Detail from a Roman fresco, Vatican Museum. First century BC

WHILE THE FAMOUS METOPE of Zeus and Hera at the Temple E in Selinus shows us, with a noble simplicity, the strength of primitive affection between husband and wife, a more recent pictorial work, of some four centuries later, *The Aldobrandini Marriage*, depicts with great delicacy and grace the feelings which attend a young bride. The ancient fresco which bears this name was discovered at the end of the sixteenth century in Rome, and first belonged to the cardinal Aldobrandini (hence the name by which it has been known ever since). It later found its way into the Vatican collection. The mural decorated a villa at the time of the emperor Augustus (at the end of the first century BC) and is in a style similar to that known as the *Second Style* in Pompeii, in whose ruins many decorative frescoes have been found. The work should not be regarded as the masterpiece of a great and original artist; unfortunately, there are no masterpieces of ancient painting in existence today as distinct from architecture and sculpture. Nevertheless, we have here a fine piece of work executed by a conscientious craftsman, who was skilled in his craft and was inspired by the famous paintings of great Greek artists of former centuries. The rich Roman who commissioned this decorative fresco to adorn a room in his large and luxurious residence in Rome, wished to see on his walls (as did all his cultured fellow-countrymen at that time) fairly faithful imitations of Greek art, which was believed to be the only art worthy of any interest. The workshops of Greek painters and sculptors, established in Rome even at the beginning of the first century BC, supplied amateurs with copies or imitations of Greek originals, to which they gave a slightly more personal character. This liking for reproductions of earlier classical art explains the lack of native Roman scenes in these paintings; they consist mainly of Greek themes, and the artist's imagination and initiative are scarcely apparent in the details of execution or even in the method of combining in a single piece of work – as was the frequent custom – two or more borrowed motifs. The workshops of this period seem to have prepared quite complete collections of the main works of art of the Hellenic period, in the form of illuminated drawings on papyrus (the same material as was used then for manuscripts). These

It is interesting to place, beside the two illustrations of marriage in Greek art (the *metope* of Selinus and *The Aldobrandini Marriage*), a monument of equal significance but of a vastly different character: the sarcophagus of Cerveteri, preserved in the Villa Giulia in Rome (Figs. 3b and 3d). It is a sculpture in terracotta which was discovered in a tomb in the Etruscan burial-ground of Cerveteri (Caere), to the west of Rome. (There is a similar sarcophagus in the Louvre in Paris.) The work dates from the second half of the sixth century BC, a time when the Etruscans, established for several centuries in central Italy, were at the height of their power.

The artist has represented an Etruscan couple stretched out, side by side, on their marriage-bed – which also served as a funerary couch – the husband behind the wife, and both leaning on their elbows in the attitude adopted by guests at a banquet in the classical era (the ancients lay on couches when participating in feasts). At a Greek banquet, however, a respectable woman would never have been seen reclining on a bed; women were seated whenever they attended banquets (something they rarely did, anyway), and it is seated in chairs that they are depicted on Greek funerary reliefs, where the man is shown reclining on a banquet-bed. It was different in Etruria: women entered freely into social life and the pleasures of company. Moreover, the Etruscans were not ashamed to depict a woman lying beside her husband on a bed when it was lying in state.

Fig. 3a. *The Aldobrandini Marriage, Italy.*

Detail from a Roman fresco, first century B.C.

3. THE ALDOBRANDINI MARRIAGE
Vatican Museum, Rome

Fig. 3b. *The Sarcophagus from Caere (detail). Etruscan, Italy. 6th century* BC.

But this effigy is not only a document on the social life and position of women; it also bears witness to the soundness and profundity of the marriage bond in an Etruscan family. This couple, reclining quietly side by side with pleasant, smiling faces, are proof of a stable, unclouded union, the foundation perhaps of a whole social structure.

The woman is friendly and gracious; the man rests his hand intimately on her shoulder in a gesture which is at once affectionate and protective. Mythological or allegorical characters are absent, for this funerary sculpture was intended simply to immortalize the memory of two human beings. However, in depicting the strength of feeling which unites them, it becomes a symbol of conjugal love.

F.C.

Fig. 3c. *Paquius Proculus and his wife. Pompeii, Italy. 1st century* BC–79 AD.

collections have apparently all disappeared; we can, however, reconstruct them with the aid of the illuminated manuscripts of the end of the ancient period. These, because they were painted on parchment, a stronger material than papyrus, have survived to this day. It is from a collection of this kind that the painter of *The Aldobrandini Marriage* drew his inspiration.

The subject illustrated, in its inspiration, composition, costumes and style, is purely Greek. The centre of the composition is occupied by the richly-draped bed, shown in three-quarter view in order to bring a feeling of depth to the picture. One of the bed-legs, made of twisted wood and bearing several carvings, is prominent in the foreground, and serves as an axis for the composition of the main group which consists of two parts which are symmetrically arranged (Fig. 3a). On the left, two damsels are seated on the bed. On the right, on a very low platform at the head of the bed sits a man. The only link between the three figures is the man's stare, which is fixed on the two women, who, deep in conversation, are unaware of anything about them. These three figures form a triangle, the lateral angles of which are at the feet of the two outer figures. The upper angle is just above the young women's heads. The arrangement, which has an immediate impact, gives a strong sense of unity to the central group.

These three characters are the principal subject of the fresco and in them is contained its full meaning. The veiled damsel, who sits in the centre on the bed, with her feet resting on a stool, is the young bride who has just entered the marriage-chamber. Her husband is not yet there. The other two figures near her are not mortals, as can be seen by their costume. While the young girl is fully-clothed, and wears a cloak or wedding-veil (which, in accordance with the Greek marriage custom, shielded her from the public gaze as she was led in procession to her husband's house), the two other figures are half-naked in a manner more fitting to the gods than to mortals. The young woman seated next to the veiled girl on the bed is a goddess of love, obviously Aphrodite herself, come down from heaven in order to comfort the young wife. She also wears a veil on her head to show that she comes as a marriage deity, but her half-naked body calls to mind the usual representation of the goddess of Love, who reveals the splendour of her body. She has placed her left hand on the bride's shoulder in a gesture of tenderness and friendship and makes a gesture of encouragement with her right hand. The group is full of charm and feeling. It derives from a long tradition in Greek art which was always concerned with depicting the feelings of tenderness between mother and daughter or two friends. There is the example (Fig. 3e) of a very beautiful funerary stele of the classical period (the end of the fifth century BC found at Rhodes, on which is shown a mother and her daughter, named Timarista and Crito, tenderly embracing each other. The group of Aphrodite and the young bride, in our fresco, is in the same tradition.

The figure seated on the right is also a god. Almost completely naked and wearing a wreath of leaves on his head, he watches the two women intently, as though impatiently awaiting the outcome of their secret conversation. He is the god Hymen, the Greek personification of marriage. He is there to preside over the marriage of the bride and groom: we know that the bridal procession sang a hymn in which they called upon Hymen to bless the new couple.

Beside this central group which is so rich in meaning, and has such a fine plastic quality, the groups on either side are of less interest. On the left, the bride's mother, draped in her ceremonial gown and holding a fan in her left hand, tests the temperature of the warm water which is being poured into a bowl by two young servant girls. A little further right, a lone figure, leaning on a column, pours the contents

Fig. 3d. *The Sarcophagus from Caere. Etruscan, Italy. 6th century* BC.

Bibliography

Amedeo Maiuri
Roman Painting
Skira, Switzerland, 1953

George M. A. Hanfmann. *Roman Art*
New York Graphic Society, Greenwich,
Connecticut. 1964

Fig. 3e. *The Camiro Stele. Rhodes. ca. 420–410* BC.

of a perfume-bottle into a kind of large shell. This semi-clothed damsel is one of the three Graces, goddesses attendant upon Aphrodite. She thus has a symbolic role in the preparation of the young bride for her marriage. Finally, on the far right is a group of three girls – friends of the bride – who take part in the wedding ceremony. One of them is sprinkling perfumed powder into a great bronze censer in order to make the air fragrant; the other two are musicians who sing the marriage anthem to the accompaniment of à lute. Thus the two outer groups, that of the mother and that of the young girls, do not participate directly in the central scene. No supernatural being figures in either of these two groups, which are completely realistic. They serve to frame the central scene and to place it within the context of a real marriage, with all its rites and established customs. The central scene, on the other hand, is placed in a world where Immortals are in authority, since these gods are charged with the task of ensuring a strong and tender union of the bride and groom.

This subtle play of symbol and allusion, resulting from the use of mythological and allegorical figures, gives a special quality to *The Aldobrandini Marriage*; the work inspires meditation in an onlooker, and deeply moves one, who, realizing its various implications, is aware of its religious solemnity, something which was, for the Greeks, inseparable from their conception of marriage. But, while the metope of Selinus lays emphasis upon the force and strength of the husband, the Roman fresco (in accordance with an era which addressed itself more willingly to the study of the feminine soul) is interested in depicting the bashfulness of the wife. It is obvious why this work, with its wealth of psychological ingenuity coupled with an excellent technique, fascinated modern artists when they were introduced to it. Rubens went into raptures over it, Van Dyck made a drawing of it, Pierre de Cortone and Poussin imitated it lovingly. This decoration for a bedroom, painted in a studio at the time of the Emperor Augustus, has been considered, for the last four centuries, one of the most moving witnesses to the genius of Hellenistic painters.

François Chamoux

4. THE MARRIAGE OF SHIVA AND PARVATI   Stone relief, early 7th century AD.
Dhumar Lena, Elura, India

The Marriage of Shiva and Parvati 4

Stone relief from the Dhumar Lena cave-temple, Elura, India. Seventh century AD

Fig. 4a. *The Demon Ravana trying to shake Shiva and Parvati off Mt. Kailasa. Khmer, Angkor Vat, Cambodia. ca. 1113–1150 AD.*

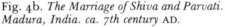

Fig. 4b. *The Marriage of Shiva and Parvati. Madura, India. ca. 7th century AD.*

THIS ROCK-CARVING of the seventh century has some of the theatrical quality of a wedding photograph. The drama takes place before our eyes, permanently transfixed in stone, an indestructible record of a momentous divine marriage. Held within the framework of an excavated rectangular panel, flanked by two large pilasters, the scene seems to be set in some great chamber. In the centre, dominating the relief, stands the four-armed Shiva, one of the gods of the great trinity of the Hindu pantheon (the two others being Brahma and Vishnu). Monumental, controlled, suffused with a quiet but deep happiness, with his principal right hand he holds the right hand of his bride, Parvati, the daughter of Himalaya, the King of the Mountains. Parvati herself, a robust, long-legged beauty, turns towards her husband, her head slightly bowed; coy and demure like any bride, she seems deeply moved at this great moment of her life. We see in this portrait of a bridal couple, carved nearly thirteen hundred years ago, a familiar and universal experience of marriage. As in any other marriage ceremony, the principal attendants are the relations and close friends of the bride and bridegroom. On Shiva's left is three-headed Brahma, the greatest and the most nebulous of the Hindu gods, the essential spirit of the Universe, 'the Basic Being'. Here he is the priest performing the wedding rituals. Behind him stands another God, perhaps Himalaya, the father of the bride, or Indra, the King of the Gods. On the other side stands Vishnu, the other member of the trinity, with his consort the goddess Lakshmi. Above and behind the gods is a host of flying deities, a multitude of wedding guests. The central figures stand out, sculpted in the round or carved in high relief. In contrast to their stillness is the activity and excitement above. The whole relief must once have been lit by oil-lamps, very much in the same way as it is lit by the photographer's lamp in our picture, throwing a highlight on the figures standing against a shadowed backdrop of rock.

To the Hindus marriage was not merely a social but a sacred institution. The wedding rites were performed by a *brahmin* priest and were little changed from the ceremony set down in the *Rig-Veda*, the ancient sacred hymns which had been given their final form early in the first millenium BC. There were three important rites in the wedding ceremony: the lighting of a sacrificial fire, to which offerings of rice and butter were made by both bride and bridegroom, a ritual oblation for the preservation of universal order; a ritual yoking to the cart, signifying both the domestic yoke and the yoke of *dharma*, the moral law; the seven steps taken hand in hand, an affirmation of mutual friendship. It is the climax of this ceremony that we see in this relief from Elura.

In Hindu art, both abstract and anthropomorphic, the artistic image is invariably the expression of a transcendental idea. The human experience is translated and transformed, often in the most sensuous terms, into a divine image. The marriage of Shiva and Parvati is not merely the celebration of the union between a god and goddess but the climax of a drama in which the salvation of the universe is at stake. In a great struggle between the gods and the demon Taraka, the gods had been badly defeated. Taraka sat on the throne of heaven and Brahma had been forced to grant him immortality, with the one limitation that he could be killed by a seven-day-old infant. Shiva, the god of creation

Fig. 4C. *The Lovers. Issurumuni Temple, Anuradhapura, Ceylon. 5–6th century* AD.

Fig. 4d. *Husband and Wife. Borobudur, Java, Indonesia, ca. 8th century* AD.

In his book, *Myths and Symbols in Indian Art and Civilization*, Heinrich Zimmer speaks of the recurrence of the God and Goddess theme in Indian art:

'In stone and bronze, again and again, this classic theme of the God and Goddess reappears, variously inflected, in the monuments of Hindu art. The God and Goddess are the first self-revelation of the Absolute, the male being the personification of the passive aspect which we know as Eternity, the female of the activating energy (*Sakti*), the dynamism of Time. Though apparently opposites they are in essence one. The mystery of their identity is stated here in symbol. She has her living counterpart in every woman as the God in every man.'

For a note on the cave-temples of Elura, see *Man through his Art,* Vol. 1, *War and Peace,* p. 27.

and destruction, was the only divinity who, through great penances and austerities, had gathered in himself the power and the energy to father such an infant. Parvati, the Daughter of the Mountains (a manifestation of the mother goddess or earth mother common to so many cultures), through her own penances and austerities was at last able to rouse him from his cosmic trance. This marriage is then the meeting of the essential male and female energies. We see in the relief not only a familiar human institution but the dramatization of a familiar mythology, the renewal of the procreative power to save the world from decay and destruction.

Senake Bandaranayake

Bibliography

Heinrich Zimmer
The Art of Indian Asia
Bollingen Series, Pantheon Books, New York, 1960

Stella Kramrisch
Art of India
Phaidon Press, London. 1965

Fig. 4e. *A donor Couple. Karli Cave Temple, India. ca. 2nd century* AD.

5 Yang Kuei-fei learning to play the flute

Silk scroll, attributed to Ch'ien Hsüan, China. c. 1235–1300

IT IS PERHAPS MORE DIFFICULT than anything else for one people to enter into the most private, intimate concepts of the life of another people. And of all such deeply personal spheres of human existence, love is surely the most abstruse, for its expression even within its native culture and idiom is one of allusion and metaphor.

In all Chinese love themes there is a dignified melancholy, a sense of helpless longing haunting even the delicate or coy, for one rarely uncovers the genuinely innocent or naïve in Chinese themes of love.

> At the time when blossoms
> Fall from the cherry-tree:
> On a day when yellow birds
> Hovered in the branches –
> You said you must stop,
> Because your horse was tired;
> I said I must go,
> Because my silkworms were hungry.

One point that stands out clearly in the Chinese literature of love and marriage, in spite of persistent orthodox pronouncements, is the frequently dominant role of woman. It is the woman who often contrives, the man who just as often acquiesces, or allows himself to pursue the ensnarement.

> There was a man so lovely,
> Clear brow well rounded.
> By chance I came across him,
> And he let me have my will.

Chinese historical imagination has always linked strong-willed ladies and their equally ardent passion for men of virtuous action or evil cunning, with the rise and fall of dynasties, with periods of sublime order and savage chaos. It is not surprising, therefore, to find as a leitmotif in much proverbial literature a cynicism toward women, to find a woman of incomparable beauty described as a 'destroyer of nations' – with a single glance, destroy a city; with two, wreck a country.

> A wise man would build a city.
> A woman, with her virtues, would destroy a city.

The greatest of all Chinese love stories, that of the Emperor Ming Huang and his consort Yang Kuei-fei, is immortalized in a long poem by an almost contemporary poet of the T'ang dynasty, Po-Chü-i. The painting attributed to Ch'ien Hsüan and reproduced here depicts a blissful moment during the long years of their deep infatuation before disaster overtook them. The emperor lovingly instructs his consort in the playing of the transverse flute while an attendant beats time with a pair of wooden clappers. Slightly apart, two court attendants express emotions rather difficult to interpret. Whether they are in a transport of delight at the sounds emanating from the flute or are reacting to the same in bemused astonishment, we cannot say. The restrained, composed, dignified vitality transmitted by gesture and facial expression, by placement of figures unifying a composition in which no coherent setting is introduced, stands in strange apposition to the voluptuous abandon of the principals' real lives.

To the Western mind, the Chinese metaphors of feminine beauty are at best repugnant.

> Her skin like pure lard,
> Her neck like white larvae of beetles,
> Her teeth like rows of melon seeds,
> Her fingers like pared onion skins,
> Her lips redder than red sulphur stones.

Yet, in spite of such formal areas of incompatible perception, there emerges here and there some hint, however fleeting, that in matters of the heart peoples of disparate cultures are not hopelessly estranged.

> I beg of you, Chung Tzu,
> Do not climb into our homestead,
> Do not break the willows we have planted.
> Not that I mind about the willows,
> But I am afraid of my father and mother.

The painting *Yang Kuei-fei learning to play the flute* is attributed to the painter Ch'ien Hsüan who was born in Chekiang province and whose life (*ca.* 1235–1300) spanned the last years of the Sung and early years of the Yüan dynasties. Ch'ien Hsüan enjoyed a reputation as a learned man which almost exceeded that of his renown as a painter during his lifetime. He declined to seek an official career, preferring to pass his days in 'leisurely poverty'.

Several contemporary writers record that his paintings were much imitated and forged during his lifetime. Among the many extant works ascribed to him, those for which the strongest arguments for authenticity may be urged reflect a concern for the reinterpretation of older modes, a cultivated archaism. The painting reproduced here, formerly in the National Museum, Peking, clearly agrees with such an estimate of the artist's work. It contains the signature of the artist and several of his personal seals.

W.T.

5. YANG-KUEI-FEI LEARNING
TO PLAY THE FLUTE
Formerly National Museum, Pekin

Attributed to Ch'ien Hsuan, *ca.* 1235-1300.
Silk scroll.

In his youth, Ming Huang, sixth emperor of the T'ang dynasty (*ca.* 713–756), was vigorous in military concerns and in the virtuous regulation of the empire. But following a visionary interview with the philosopher Lao-tzu (sixth century BC) in 741, and especially after his demoralizing infatuation with Yang Kuei-fei, he abandoned himself more and more to luxury and extravagant revelry, ennobled the members of his consort's family and finally virtually abdicated royal responsibility to the corrupt and selfish greed of this clan. 'Whenever they (Yang Kuei-fei and a sister, Lady Kuo-kuo) came to pay a visit they would pound along the road together with a hundred or more ladies-in-waiting galloping after; torches so close together that it seemed like day; face-powder enough to fill a mile, and not a curtain or screen

Figs. 5a and 5b. *A Couple. Korea. 18th century (?)*

closed (for modesty) anywhere.' The unparalleled extravagance of their lives and passion was everything which those steeped in orthodox Confucian propriety would have found distasteful . . .

> In a gold house she adorned herself for the night,
> In jade towers after feasts they were harmoniously drunk with spring.

and as such they would have held them to be offensive in the light of the ideal of the proper sovereign.

The tragic end of this love affair was precipitated not through moral remonstrances, but through the treachery of a man both emperor and consort had favoured and rewarded with intimacy and high station. An Lu-shan was of Turkish descent. Legends of marvels surround the story of his birth. His bold exploits as a frontier warrior, his magnificent stature and exotic appearance, his quick and ingratiating repartee, his readiness to breach convention appealed to the lovers' own reckless indulgence and he became a favourite of Ming Huang. Flattered by his extravagant gallantry toward her, Yang Kuei-fei called him her adopted son. Possibly rash but sincere in the beginning, earnest and brave, irrational, ambitious and easily inflamed, An Lu-shan became, perhaps by the excessive doting of the court, inflated with pride and greed, and in the year 756 he unleashed a revolt against the already tottering throne. Ming Huang and his consort were forced to flee their palace in Ch'ang-an, and along their road to exile the mutinous soldiers demanded the lives of Yang Kuei-fei and several of the corrupt members of her family whom they held responsible for the catastrophe which had so precipitously befallen the country.

> Turning helplessly, eyebrows perished before the horses,
> Hairpins scattered over the ground – no one retrieves them,
> Kingfisher feathers, gold birds, jade hairpins . . .
> The emperor hid his face, unable to save her.
> When he turned to look, tears of blood streamed down.

The revolt was crushed, but Ming Huang never regained his throne. An Lu-shan was slain by his own son who feared he would not succeed his father to the throne which was never won. Ming Huang lived the last few lonely years of his life in constant despair for his precious consort.

> Days there were when peach and pear bloomed in the spring sun.
> And a time when the leaves of the wu-t'ung fell in autumn rains.
> By the West and South Palaces thick are the autumn grasses,
> Fallen leaves, unswept, fill the steps with red.

And the pathetic hope born of that grief was expressed by the poet Po Chü-i in an image of universal longing of separated lovers:

> In the heavens we shall be twin birds in flight,
> On earth we shall be two trees whose branches entwine.

William Trousdale

Bibliography

James Cahill
'Ch'ien Hsüan and his Figure Paintings'
Archives of the Chinese Art Society of America
Vol. XII (1958) pp. 10–28 (trans.) Witter Bynner

The Jade Mountain
Po-Chü-i, 'Song of Unending Sorrow'
New York, 1945

6. CHRIST AND ST. JOHN

Stuftun Preussischer Kulturbesitz
Staatlich Museum, Berlin Dahlem

German, ca. 1320.
Gilded polycrome oak carving. 34½ × 17½ in. : 89 × 45 cm.

Christ and St. John 6

Gilded polychrome oak carving, Swabia, Germany. c. 1320

LOVE IS THE UNION between two persons; it may be consummated in the union of man and woman but it may also exist between father and son, between two brothers and even between friends. It is sometimes experienced almost mysteriously by two people who meet suddenly, apparently by accident – on a journey, in an inn by the roadside – and who find one another in a few moments of complete understanding. Such an experience of love, by its very nature, remains silent; it wells up within us as a feeling of bliss, unexpected, unfathomable, and complete.

The wood carving in Plate 6 has much of the naïve simplicity of folk art and its meaning is quite clear: it is an expression of love. Two human beings are seated together so closely that the gentle rhythm pervading their bodies and garments blends them into a single form. One of the two, smaller than the other, is a very young man, almost an adolescent. He has fallen asleep as a boy might on a long journey. His head is leaning over, resting against the shoulder and chest of his companion; his right hand, in a touching and tender gesture of trust, is resting in that of his friend. The older man has put his left hand lightly on the youth's shoulder, and gently holds the right hand of the sleeper whom he does not wish to awaken. The bearded head of the older man is slightly inclined towards the left. The expression on his face is grave, as if from knowledge of some approaching doom of which the sleeper is unaware. The relationship between the two is expressed not only in the heads and hands but in the attitudes of the figures as a whole. Every fold of the boy's garment seems to describe that abandon, confidence, and unconscious trust with which his entire body leans over against his friend. Penetrating into the secret stillness of sleep, the work seems to reveal an experience far deeper than rational understanding. The older man on the other hand, while united with his companion in tender affection, is obviously the protector; all the lines of the composition flow from his head which is raised above the group with grave significance; it is as if his head shelters the other's sleep, and the soft ripples with which the older man's garment is spread over the knees of the sleeper seem to convey their silent communion as eloquently as does the meeting of their hands.

The group depicts Christ and Saint John, the disciple 'whom Christ loved'. Its scriptural source is a brief passage in the account of the last supper according to the Gospel of St. John (13 : 23):

> 'But there was one among the disciples who sat at the table on the breast of Jesus whom Jesus loveth. . . .'

During centuries of Christian thought these few words grew into a legend. John was thought to have been the bridegroom of the Wedding at Cana who, after Christ had miraculously changed water into wine, left his bride to follow the Master. On the island of Patmos, in the Mediterranean, John, as a very old man, wrote down the tremendous vision of things to come which, as the Book of Revelation, became the final part of the Bible. There were many who believed that the vision had been revealed to the youthful Saint John in a dream precisely at that moment in the Last Supper when he had fallen asleep leaning on the Lord's breast.

For Christian thought John remained the 'bridal' disciple, the only one of the twelve whom Christian art depicted as a youth. As the disciple whom Christ loved, he came to embody the union of every Christian soul with God. Indeed we may consider our group an image of the religious attitude that in the later part of the Middle Ages, replaced the fear of God by the love of God; in the words of St. Bernard of Clairvaux, the greatest spokesman of this attitude: 'God has become your brother'.

This experience is embodied in our wood carving. It obviously alludes to the scene at the Last Supper mentioned above, but it is much more than a detail from, or an abridged version of, that event. In very small dimensions the isolated group of Christ and the beloved disciple had since the twelfth century occasionally appeared in miniatures. Later the theme was treated in a number of wood carvings (of which Plate 6 is the most beautiful), all closely related, all created within a few decades of the early fourteenth century and within the narrowly defined region of Swabia in south-western Germany. After that the group vanished again. None of the rare imitations of later periods which have survived have grasped the spirit of the earlier group.

We do not know the exact circumstances in which our group came into existence, but for our understanding of it, it is quite sufficient to realise how wonderfully it conveys the mystical union between the soul and God. Medieval thought had found in *The Song of Songs*, the Old Testament collection of love poems by King Solomon, the most eloquent literary expression of that experience. The verse, 'I sleep but my heart waketh in Thee', is quoted again and again in this context by medieval writers. The passage evokes that complete abandonment, that ultimate surrender, confidence, and tenderness which is the hallmark and secret of love.

This mystical sleep is the theme of our wood carving. We can but marvel how the artist has conveyed so delicate, so unfathomable a sentiment in a composition simple and naïve like a folk song. It has been remarked that a contrast seems to exist between, on the one hand, the treatment of the heads and hands, and on the other, the 'coarseness' of the feet and garments. This interpretation is erroneous; the hands as such are shaped as crudely as the feet; and the facial expressions, hair and beard are carved with the same simple flow which we note in the folds of the garments.

A more sophisticated treatment could only have weakened the gentle power with which the group expresses its theme, bestowing upon it the unchallengeable simplicity of man's deepest insights.

Otto von Simson

Fig 6a. *St. John (detail).*

Bibliography

Hans Wentzel
Die Christus—Johannes Gruppen des XIV Jahrhunderts
Stuttgart, 1960

لااغنئ فلمّاحضّرالقاضي وكان ممّن يرئ فضّل الامساك وبقُصّ ثفانه السواحتّابو ذبيس

7. ABU ZAYD AND HIS WIFE
Bibliothèque Nationale, Paris

Al-Wasiti 1237.
Manuscript illustrations. Approx. actual size.

Abu Zayd and his Wife 7

Illustrations by al-Wasiti to a manuscript of al-Hariri's 'Makamat', Baghdad, Iraq. 1237

The story of Abu Zayd and the Kadi of Alexandria is related in the ninth *Makamat*. Abu Zayd's young and attractive wife complains to the Kadi, who is a kind and good-natured man, that Abu Zayd married her under false pretences, saying that he was rich, but in fact was so poor he could scarcely maintain her. The Kadi threatens to imprison him. Abu Zayd so eloquently pleads his defence, saying that the riches he claimed to have had were his 'pearls of thought' which he hoped to 'string into elegant poems to earn money from rich and poor' but as times were so bad trade had fallen off. The Kadi is so moved by his speech that he gives him money and sends him on his way. The Kadi later learns from his friend al-Harith (the narrator who appears in each of the Abu Zayd stories often as friend and adviser to both Abu Zayd and his victim) that the whole thing was in fact a trick to make him part with his money. He replies, good-natured man that he is, that Abu Zayd's defence was so brilliant and so beautifully constructed that the entertainment was well worth the money he had lost.

The fortieth 'Makamat', one of the most entertaining stories in the collection, tells the story of Abu Zayd and his wife pleading before the Kadi of Tabriz. Abu Zayd accuses his wife of persistent disobedience. 'I married her', he says, 'that she might make me forgetful of exile and cleanse me from the squalor of celibacy.' But she has failed him, refuses to obey him and has made him poor, tired and hungry. He asks that he be given a divorce or that some settlement be brought about. His wife in turn argues that he is an old and pitiable creature, hardly able to maintain her. They both make long and abusive but well-argued pleas. The Kadi, who is well-known for his meanness and his parsimony, is utterly confused and unable to decide between the claims, and is reluctantly forced to give them each a gold coin as compensation for their respective difficulties. He suspects throughout that he is being tricked, but the arguments are so brilliant that he sees no other way out of it than to compensate them both. Having sent them on their way, he is so upset at the thought of having had to part with his money that he closes the court for the day.

THE ADVENTURES OF ABU ZAYD, the rascally but lovable hero of the *Makamat* who wanders from city to city earning his living by his brilliant wit and eloquence, were originally designed as an exercise in language (see *Man through his Art*, Vol. 4, *Education*, Plate 7). The stories, however, apart from their ingenious combinations of rhyme, rhythm, pun and riddle, are a wide canvas on which is vividly portrayed the life of the contemporary Islamic world. Our illustrations here show Abu Zayd and his young wife appearing before the *Kadis*, or Judges, of Alexandria and Tabriz. In the first picture we see Abu Zayd prostrating himself before the Kadi of Alexandria, while his wife complains about him. From what we can see of her sharp gestures we have an impression of a certain kind of woman, fat and slow, and yet quick to rebuke and long-complaining. Abu Zayd himself appears as a cunning, obsequious old man willing to go to any lengths to gain his ends. He is probably afraid of his wife and makes a great show of being impressed and intimidated by the authority of the Kadi. The Kadi, as he is seen in the painting though not in the actual story itself, is certainly a stern and authoritative figure, with his elaborate headdress and robes and his boldly designed throne. By the side of the Kadi, appearing as a kind of eavesdropper, his eyes alight with curiosity, is another figure who probably represents al-Harith, the narrator of the *Makamat* and a clearly defined personality in the Abu Zayd stories. In the other picture, it is Abu Zayd who complains to the Kadi of Tabriz about his wife. His mournful face, his downcast eyes and his dark robes so expressively portray the aggrieved husband, while his wife sits behind him, bored, impatient and quite unintimidated. The mean and parsimonious Kadi of Tabriz listens carefully to Abu Zayd and seems to be convinced, though reluctantly, by Abu Zayd's story. The figure of the narrator, again, stands beside the Kadi, with a look of exaggerated withdrawal and slightly amused satisfaction on his face.

Al-Wasiti's paintings reflect so expressively, in their own pictorial terms, the satire, wit and rich characterization of the *Makamat*. Drawn with economy, they present us with familiar human situations and a dramatic humour which is immediately appealing. As we can see from the stories themselves (see note), there is no real estrangement between Abu Zayd and his wife. It is one of his many tricks, entirely contrived between him and his wife in order to give him an opportunity to use his eloquence and wit, and to use his powers of persuasion to obtain money from his listeners, through their admiration or sympathy. To this extent then the paintings and the stories are not direct portrayals of marriage, but a genuine parody of it, in which Abu Zayd and his wife are the principal actors and the Kadis the unsuspecting participants.

The Arabs, like all other peoples, knew only too well the difficulties and the disagreeable features of married life. But marriage was regarded almost universally in Islam as a positive duty and its neglect was subject to severe reproach. Children were greatly treasured and sons especially were thought to be a gift from God. A wife's first duty consisted of service to her husband, the care of her children and the management of her household. Her spare time would be spent in spinning and weaving. She was seen little in public, because by about the end of the tenth century the system of strict seclusion and the segregation of the sexes had become general.

The attitude of the Arabs towards women has always been chivalrous. This was never more so than in the Middle Ages when the high position and general esteem which women enjoyed in the Arab world greatly influenced certain aspects of chivalry in the Christian world. Arabian poetry made frequent mention of the virtues of the Arab mistress, virtues which were very similar to those of the Roman matron. Proud, chaste, pure, insisting on her husband and sons being men and not cowards, she presents a picture of a resolute person, completely dedicated to the comfort and welfare of her family.

If one regards the copious flood of Arabic love poetry (expressed in lines of intense passion and exquisite felicity) as a criterion, one may assume that many an Arab lady was suffused in the rich perfumes of romantic love. The Arabian ideals of female beauty required that a woman's stature should be like the bamboo among plants, her face as round as the full moon, her hair darker than night and her cheeks white and rosy.

Though polygamy was practised throughout the Arab world, being sanctioned by the Prophet Mohammed himself, it was a strict principle that there should be equality and a fair division between the several wives. It was usually an upper class phenomenon as it was required that a man should be in a position to maintain each of his several wives at the same level of emotional and material well-being as he could one wife. In later periods, when a social decline had set in, concubinage became increasingly prevalent and very soon, especially among the upper classes, the *harem* began to gain prominence over the domestic hearth.

The Editors

For short notes on Arab painting and on the *Makamat* (The Assemblies) of al-Hariri, see *Man through his Art*, Vol. 4, *Education*, Plate 7.

Fig. 7a. Abu Zayd's wife pleads before the Kadi of Tabriz. Baghdadi School, Iraq.

8. THE ARNOLFINI MARRIAGE

National Gallery, London

Jan van Eyck, 1434.

Oil painting on wood. 33 × 22½ in. : 83.8 × 57 cm.

The Arnolfini Marriage 8

Oil painting on wood, by Jan van Eyck, Flemish School, Netherlands. 1434

Fig. 8a. *The Arnolfini Marriage (detail).*

Jan van Eyck was born *c.* 1390 and died at Bruges (in modern Belgium) in 1441. Jan van Eyck stands at the head of the Flemish painters of the fifteenth century, who represent the most remarkable flowering of late medieval art in Northern Europe. Van Eyck also worked as a miniaturist and in 1425 was employed as court painter by the Duke of Burgundy. Later he settled in Bruges (a cosmopolitan commercial centre) and was often commissioned by its rich merchants and citizens. One of the great European masters, he improved on the already existing technique of painting in oils and had a command of perspective which equalled that of his Italian contemporaries.

Bibliography

E. Panofsky
Jan van Eyck's Arnolfini Portrait
Burlington Magazine 64, 1934

E. Panofsky
Jan van Eyck's Arnolfini Portrait
Burlington Magazine 64, 1934

H. Kauffmann
Jan van Eyck's Arnolfinihochzeit'
Vierteljahresschrift fur Kultur und Geisteswissenschaft, Vol. 4, 1950

Max J. Friedländer. *From van Eyck to Bruegel: Early Netherlandish Painting*
Phaidon Press, London, 1965

THE ARNOLFINI MARRIAGE, by Jan van Eyck, is perhaps the supreme visual statement of the meaning of Christian marriage in western art. We are captivated by its haunting ambivalence: we find ourselves in a room warmly familiar, yet at the same time there is something inexpressibly strange, not only about the attitude of the man and woman before us, but also about the stillness and clarity of every object that meets our eye.

We know that the painting is the marriage portrait of an Italian merchant, Giovanni Arnolfini, and his wife, Giovanna Cenami. But Jan van Eyck has given us much more than a portrait. He has revealed the mysterious meaning of Christian marriage itself. We must recall that, for the Christian, marriage is a sacrament, in theological language, a 'visible sign of God's invisible Grace' bestowed upon husband and wife as their union is consummated. Christian marriage according to the words of St. Paul is also the mystical image of the union between Christ and his Church. Jan van Eyck unfolds before our eyes the meaning of this entire experience (that which links the visible and the invisible worlds) precisely by making us see all the familiar things of this world in a light which transfigures them. He speaks to us on two levels: first of all he records in a matter-of-fact way the marriage ceremony as it occurred: the husband and wife joining hands, the husband raising his right hand, pronouncing his marriage vow. To make the ceremony valid there has to be a witness; as we look closely into the mirror on the wall, we see, between the couple, two figures. The painter, by the beautifully written inscription has made explicit their identity; 'Jan van Eyck was here'; in other words, the artist himself acted as witness and commemorated this fact in his painting.

The Christian marriage, we have said, is a sacrament consummated by husband and wife. The artist has indicated this by choosing the marital chamber as his setting; yet he has bestowed upon every visible object a mystical meaning, which his contemporaries could immediately understand. The sandals recall the biblical scene where Moses was asked by God to take off his shoes: so they attest the presence of God in this bridal chamber. The dog is an image of fidelity. The single light burning in the chandelier is the symbol of Christ. The little carved figure on the marriage bed represents St. Margaret, a saint invoked by women in childbirth. Note the beautiful harmony between the curve described by the arms of the couple and the mirror, the frame of which is adorned with ten tiny scenes representing the Passion of Christ. What matters is not the presence and meaning of all these symbols as such, but rather the artist's ability to make us feel that behind all these objects, seemingly so familiar to our daily experience, we can grasp a reality, at once mysterious and all-pervading; that this reality bestows its meaning upon the scene we are witnessing, imparting even to the fifteenth century bourgeois bedchamber the hallowed twilight of a sanctuary. In a way, every great work of art joins the two realities of our existence. But no artist seems to have been quite able to imitate the achievement of Jan van Eyck in this evocation of Christian Marriage.

Otto von Simson

9 The Two Lovers

Tempera on wood; Swabian School, Ulm, Germany. c. 1460–1470.

THOUGH THIS PICTURE is one of two lovers, it is thought that it is actually an engagement picture, that is to say, relating to two definite individuals, a citizen of repute in his town of Ulm and his bride to be. However, the two lovers are placed in the setting of a garden and the artist uses many of the conventions and symbols that were found in the pictures of lovers of an earlier tradition; the similarity in dress, the flower symbols and the garden setting.

The two lovers in this panel stand half facing each other; the young man, stepping forward, presents a small blue flower (probably wild chicory, a favourite of love magic) to his lady. She is dressed in a rose coloured gown, the skirt of which she gathers into folds at her waist, revealing a green lining and white undergown. Her flowing golden hair is bound with a diadem and she wears a jewelled brooch on her gown. The youth wears a red and white tunic; the upper garment has a green panel down the front. His hair is also flowing and golden, and in his gold diadem he wears the same blue flower he is offering to his lady. The pair of lovers wear one sleeve of the same brown foliated damask, it being a custom of the age of chivalry for a gentleman to have a sleeve of his tunic to match one worn by his lady.

The flower symbolism is complex, containing allusions to both love and death: roses, wild cherry, white currant, buttercups, clover, dandelions, lilies of the valley, Solomon's seal . . . . . and the lovers, against this tapestry-like leafy background, stand out radiant and luminous.

In the Museum at Strasbourg there is a panel of almost exactly the same measurements showing two decayed bodies, with toads and vipers. This panel was once the reverse panel of *The Two Lovers*. They undoubtedly belong together as a love and death allegory. The bridegroom was obviously well-off and somewhat over-dressed – notice his 'garter' of pearls and golden ornaments. The bride seems dressed more simply. This is quite understandable as men in the Middle Ages dressed more fancifully than women. But the similarities of colour

The painting of *The Two Lovers* is by an associate of the great Swabian painter Mieltsher and seems to have been painted *ca.* 1460–1470 AD.

Fig. 9a. *The Marriage of Peace and Love. Tapestry, Touraine, France. early 16th century.*

9. THE TWO LOVERS

The Cleveland Museum of Art, Ohio

Swabian School, ca. 1460-1470.

Tempera on wood. 25½ × 15½ in. : 64.7 × 39 cm.

Fig. 9b. *The Betrothed. The Master of the Housebook, Swabian School, Germany. ca. 1480.*

Fig. 9c. *The Offering of the Heart. French Tapestry, 15th century.*

Bibliography

The Bulletin of the Cleveland Museum of Art
Cleveland, Ohio, 1932

Th. Musper
'Ein Ulmer Verlöbnisbild'
Die Kunst, Vol. 47, 1949

A. Stange
Deutsche Malerei der Gotik, Vol. 8
Munich, 1957

in their robes and their brown damask sleeves is more a symbolic than a colouristic device.

The subject of *The Two Lovers* appealed to popular sentiment; the tapestries (Fig. 9c), prints and drawings of the time show that this subject was a favourite one. There are many similar couples in the love-feast tapestries from South Germany and Switzerland. An anonymous engraver and painter known as the Master of the Housebook, a contemporary of Martin Schongauer, also worked in Swabia and his painting of a Pair of Lovers or *The Betrothed* in the Gotha Museum (Fig. 9b) shows similarities in facial expression, hair, eyes, noses and chins, but the costumes and general treatment show it to be of a later date.

The Editors

10 'Le Cuer d'Amour Espris' (The Heart Possessed by Love)

Miniature paintings from an illuminated manuscript, France. 1465

THE ILLUMINATED MANUSCRIPT OF *The Heart Possessed by Love* in the Vienna National Library is a strange and wonderful book, surprising at first in the contrast between its medieval form and content and the intensely modern spirit apparent in the beauty of its miniatures and their methods of plastic expression. They anticipate in several instances the romantic sensibility and the completely new conception of landscape painting which is yet to come. The poem itself was written by King René of the House of Anjou, who was also the author of the *Book of Tournaments* and *The Humiliation of Empty Pleasure*. It is also possible that he was a painter and that he himself illustrated some of the books he wrote (see note).

The Humiliation is the earlier of the two allegorical romances, the other being the present work. It is dedicated to René's first wife, Isabella of Lorraine, whose death he mourned in 1453. It is a dialogue between the King's Soul and his Heart; the soul, inspired by mystic love, reproaching Heart for having lost himself in earthly vanities, 'empty pleasure'. One sees in this book the old tradition of a 'trial', the moral and spiritual debate, which endeavoured to turn man away from earthly delights in order to direct his eyes solely towards heaven.

However, several years later the inconsolable widower of *The Humiliation* fell in love with and married Jeanne de Laval in whose honour he composed *The Heart Possessed by Love*, in which she appears as Sweet Mercy (*Douce Mercy*). Of the text itself there is little to be said here. It is a story of chivalry and adventure, a fairy-tale, and may be thought of as the 'quest' for Sweet Mercy, a voyage of discovery, culminating in the possession of love, of the beloved, of wisdom and of knowledge. The visionary journeys, which were often only pastimes, sometimes filled with an esoteric or mystic sense, were very popular in the Middle Ages when, on account of pilgrimages and crusades, not to speak of trade, people travelled a great deal more than is believed of them today. Despite the fascinating period of the Renaissance in which he lived, rich as it was in discoveries, King René, like many of his illustrious contemporaries, turned to this medieval world which in time had come to be painted in sumptuous and stirring colours (see note).

The scheme of the poem adheres closely to the tradition of medieval allegorical romances and features well-known characters like Care (*Souci*), Jealousy (*Jalousie*), Idleness (*Paresse*), Hope (*Esperance*), and Melancholy (*Mélancolie*), some of whom guide the lover towards his lady, while others set snares along the difficult and dangerous route he has to travel in order to reach Sweet Mercy's castle. The two heroes of the tale are Heart (the lover) and Desire (his squire). Apart from the miniatures, commissioned by King René from an unknown artist (thought to have been possibly Coppin Delft, Bartholomew de Clerc, or the King himself, for want of a precise identification), the poem alone is of no great interest. The magic of this magnificent and fascinating book comes from the real and, at the same time, fantastic world so vividly evoked by the painter.

Even if the painter respects the medieval conventions imposed by the poem itself he projects them into a world so new, so astonishing that it is no longer even that of the Renaissance. He proclaims an age, still far off, when there will be an immediate, acute and sensuous con-

Fig. 10a. *Portrait of King René. Miniature from a Latin Ms., France. 15th century.*

The author of *The Heart Possessed by Love* was King René of the House of Anjou, Count of Provence, King of Sicily and Jerusalem. He was a strange and interesting person, a patron of the arts who possessed both a Renaissance spirit of inquiry and a kind of nostalgia for the Middle Ages. The author of the *Book of Tournaments* and two allegorical romances, *The Humiliation of Empty Pleasure* and *The Heart Possessed by Love*, it is also possible that he had studied painting during the long period of captivity he underwent at Dijon, in the Tour de Bar where he had been imprisoned by his political opponent Philip the Good, Duke of Burgundy, Grand Duke of the West. He may himself have illustrated the *Book of Tournaments* and perhaps even *The Heart Possessed by Love*.

One of King René's whims was to revive tournaments at a time when true chivalry had fallen into a decline and little more than the external form of its past grandeur remained. He set forth the rules, the ritual and, one might even say, a liturgy, in his *Book of Tournaments*. In *The Heart Possessed by Love* he restored to favour the amorous quest, dear to the stories of Chivalry of the preceding centuries, when the tradition of courtly

10. LE CUER D'AMOUR ESPRIS
Osterreichische Nationalbibliothek, Vienna

French, 1465.
Miniature paintings approx. actual size.

love also prevailed, as with the German *Minnesang*. The idioms of Sacred Love and Profane Love were often interchanged as in the *Song of Songs* and the erotic Islamic poems, which had such a great influence on the Provençals and perhaps even on the *sweet new style* of Dante and his Italian contemporaries. *The Heart Possessed by Love* is dominated by René's desire to bring to life again a world long since dead, yet reveals all his forebodings of a new world about to overthrow completely the old order of things.

The two-fold relationship with the Middle Ages on the one hand and the Renaissance and post-Renaissance world on the other is felt even in the illustrations themselves. We find a form of Romanticism in the dread cult of the forest, in the great trees, dense and gloomy, stretching as far as the eye can see in the Forest of Long-Waiting (*Long-Attente*) at the edge of which stands the manor (Renaissance in structure and decoration) where Jealousy lives. Of the same nature, too, is the supernatural dawn which lights up Heart's morning prayer before the Fountain of Fortune.

At the same time, the characters themselves are highly individualized and sometimes naïve and over-exaggerated in a form of stage-illusion as in medieval mystery plays. Idleness appears in a torn, open gown, her shoes unlaced and her hair dishevelled; Jealousy, a barbarous shrew and almost a beast, is clothed in animal skins; grey-gowned Melancholy wails in front of a miserable, half-dead fire, beneath a thatched roof. All this had its place in the imagery of the Middle Ages, when allegories were more popular than they were subtle. The painter of *The Heart Possessed by Love* has not had recourse to an obscure esotericism; the symbolism remains simple and immediately comprehensible as though the painter wished to remain faithful to the usual clarity of the Gothic image-makers.

M.B.

The cult of 'Fin Amor', of True Love, evolved in the twelfth century in Southern France. With its dramatis personae (the knight, the lady and the 'gilos' or husband lurking in the background) and its over-riding concern with the state of the lover's heart, it soon became a commonplace of the troubadours and jongleurs, the lyric poets and journeyman singers of Provence who gave it a great elaboration of form. One of its principal literary devices was personification: Love, Mercy, Fear, Jealousy and countless others held debates and quarrelled among themselves within the poet's heart. The *Roman de la Rose* cycle is an outstanding example of the literature produced within this convention.

ception of nature, at times almost Impressionistic. The Master of *The Heart Possessed by Love* was not content with the unworldly landscapes of his predecessors: he wished to depict so perfectly the hour of the day, the season, the temperature and the climate, that it is easy to recognize the familiar scenery of Touraine, where this book was obviously compiled by an artist of the School of Tours.

The splendid nocturnal sea-scene where Betrothal and Hope accompany Heart and Desire in their boat which they are to take to the island where Fellowship and Goodwill dwell (Plate 10 (i)); the romance of the night, profound and harmonious like the Night of Creation, which surrounds the sleeping travellers; the sunset, of purple, blue and gold, when they are knocking at the door of the Hermitage in the forest—all this is quite new, and indicates a conception of landscape-painting which enbraces both the fantastic realism of the Romantics and the liveliness of the visual sensation of the Impressionists, faithfully rendered with a preciseness and freshness of manner.

The artist was primarily concerned with the inner conflict of the main characters, Heart and Desire, and, instead of wild and tragic scenes, he has depicted a quiet gravity, often even a complete immobility, which gives emphasis to those moments when the characters are deeply moved in this enchanted world. In order to convey to a spectator the new sense of time to which the travellers submit once they cross the frontier between our world and the enchanted world, the painter sets each episode in an arrested moment, when, literally, time is stopped by the use of magic, or because, as they change place, time is also changed for them.

In order to obtain such new, striking and varied luminous effects, the painter had to adopt a new use of colour and use it for methods of

Fig. 10b. *The Declaration of Love. Pillar Capital from the Ducal Palace, Venice, att. to Serolo Lombardo.*

expression which were different from the colour symbolism inherited from the Middle Ages. In particular, his use of light and shade – which was to become the baroque quality par excellence – plays an important part in these miniatures of the mid-fifteenth century. In the second scene (Plate 10 (ii)) where Love entrusts the King's Heart to Ardent Desire (*Vif Désir*), two sources of light focus their beams on the encounter – the red heart torn from the breast of the sleeping king and the lamp, half-hidden under a small table. This effect, often used by Altdorfer and Lucas de Leyde, and which was to figure frequently in the tableaux of Adam Elseheimer, is employed here as well, as a device to evoke emotion in a dramatic and even theatrical sense, but it emphasizes equally the supernatural side of this story, the slipping away from normal space and time.

The Master of *The Heart Possessed by Love* makes use of light in two ways: realistically, to indicate time and place, with complete fidelity to the visual impression; and unrealistically, or surrealistically, to suggest the passing of the objective world, and highlight the different reality of a dream, of a vision, of the supernatural experience undergone by the character in the secret place of his heart, as a stage in his approach to the infinite, the absolute, the sublime. In such a way, the enchanted night is depicted, when the travellers fall asleep by the Fountain of Fortune, over which the dawn rises with long shadows. There, while Ardent Desire is still wrapped in restless and sensuous sleep, Heart offers up a prayer and meditates in the increasingly dazzling rays of the sun.

The quasi-impressionistic method of indicating the time of each episode and the descriptions of fresh meadows and Touraine woods are intensified by the extraordinary poetry of the light in which each scene is bathed. It is a fine and fluid light – of a transparent and vibrant quality in the daytime episodes, and heavy with strangeness and mystery when night plunges the travellers into darkness, in which Heart's silver armour and winged helmet glitter fantastically. As far as the heroes' faces are concerned, they bear the characteristic features of the human type they personify. In Heart's face can be seen that expression of dreamy emotion and visionary passion which pursues earthly happiness in the same way that one would seek to possess the delights of paradise. Heart is the knight par excellence of the stories of the Round Table, where he has his place between Galahad and Gawain. Desire is also an image of love, but he can only *follow* the ideal love, the pure love which Heart embodies. As his name indicates, and as is further borne out by the flames embroidered on his white tunic, he is consumed by a desire for earthly, sensual pleasure. His face, too, tormented, pathetic and violent, speaks of the vehemence of his carnal interests. In the same way that the poems of Orpheus define man as being *a child of the earth and the sky*, so King René, author and real hero of this book, displays himself in the two characters who are each motivated in the quest by different aims and whose different personalities point to both a platonic and a sensual aspect of the same individual. The companions, brought together in the same adventure, the idealist and the voluptuary, are inseparable, although at no point equal. Desire is dependent upon Heart; he obeys and serves him, always following him at a suitable distance, but his presence is also necessary to the success of the venture. Thus they go along together, across the symbolic forest, the heroes of an amorous adventure which takes them into various spheres of human society and to lands where a young soul expands and sings.

Marcel Brion

Fig. 10c. *Herzog Heinrich von Breslau at a tournament. German Minnesinger Miniature. Late 13th century.*

Disapproved of by the Church, it was suppressed in Southern France in the thirteenth century, but by this time it had taken root in the north and in Italy. The main stream of the tradition as it was handed down to the Renaissance was carried on by Petrarch in the fourteenth century. In his Rime he included all the traditional equipment of the troubadours and made it readily accessible, not only to his fellow countrymen but to all the poets of the new vernacular tongues which were just coming into their own throughout Europe.

The Heart Possessed by Love is a splendid elaboration of the allegory of personified emotions, each dealing in their turn with the lover's heart. The conventional landscape, carefully observed and represented with detailed precision, conveys a sense of timelessness by the use of traditional characters familiar to its audience.

Bibliography

E. Trenkler
Das Livre du Cuer d'Amour Espris
Vienna. 1947/8

O. Paecht
'René d'Anjou et les van Eyck'
Cahiers de l'Assoc. Internat. des Etudes Françaises Paris. 1956

11. MAJNUN BROUGHT IN CHAINS TO LAYLA'S TENT
British Museum

Mir Sayyid Ali, 1539-1543.
Miniature painting. 12 ⅞ × 7 ⅝ in. : 32.7 × 19 cm.

Majnun brought in Chains to Layla's Tent 11

Miniature painting by Mir Sayyid Ali, Tabriz, Persia. 1539–1543

This miniature illustrated in our plate is from a sumptuous manuscript made for the Persian ruler Shah Tahmasp between the years 1539 and 1543 at his capital Tabriz. Many of the greatest painters of the day contributed fourteen of its seventeen miniatures, the remaining three being seventeenth century additions. Among them was Mir Sayyid Ali, the artist of the miniature illustrated here. He was the son of the painter Mir Musavvir and one of the leading painters of the court *atelier* at Tabriz. Within a few years of painting this miniature, he was presented to Humayun, the Mughal Emperor of India then in exile in Persia, and when the latter recovered his kingdom Mir Sayyid Ali followed him to India where he and another Persian painter, Abd us-Samad, founded the Mughal School of Indian painting (see note to Plate 14).

The miniature of *Layla and Majnun at School* (Fig. 11a) comes from a manuscript of Nizami's Khamsa copied in 1442 AD. All except one of its miniatures were added later. Most, including the one illustrated here, were painted at Herat, capital of the last great Timurid ruler of Persia about the year 1493. Three of the miniatures are the work of Persia's greatest painter, Bihzad, and many of the others, such as that illustrated, must have been painted by his pupils.

The scene is laid in a mosque school, as is indicated by the *mimbar* or tall stepped pulpit and the *mihrab* or arched prayer niche preceded by a dome. The arch and back wall are adorned with splendid coloured tile mosaic, a feature of Persian architecture at this period. At the back, the young Qais and Layla exchange glances before the suspicious eyes of an old duenna. The painting gives a vivid picture of a school: one pupil is writing, another reads aloud to the old schoolmaster. The artist has paid particular attention to detail, such as the writing implements, penbox, books and bookstand, furniture and carpet.

Fig. 11b is an example of the way in which the Mughal painters of India treated the Layla and Majnun theme. The manuscript from which it is taken was copied in 1558 and its five miniatures were executed probably by one hand between 1600 and 1610. The incident

A PEOPLE'S ASPIRATIONS are embodied in its art and literature and in its folklore. The chivalrous virtues sung by the Arabs in the Days of Ignorance became the ideals of conduct in Islamic society. Fidelity in friendship and constancy in love were lauded as much as courage and generosity. In the pre-Islamic poetry of Arabia, the love theme came to be an essential element in the *qasida* or ode which was required by convention to open with an erotic prelude known as the *nasib*. The poet rides solitarily past the deserted spring encampment and recalls the carefree days which he once spent there in the company of his beloved.

At about the time of the coming of Islam, sentimental love was yielding place to a highly romantic conception of love inspired by the tribe of Udhra who 'die of their love'. This idea, that the most perfect love is that which remains unfulfilled, is expressed by an unknown poet.

> Three be the ways of love: a knitting of heart to heart, a pleasing of lips and eyes: a third love whose name is Death.

Such a notion is sanctioned even by the Prophet Mohammed whom tradition credits with the saying, 'he who loves but remains chaste, never reveals his secret and dies, dies the death of a martyr'. Thus 'Udhri love' became the ideal of conduct in love for the *adib*, the truly cultivated man of Islamic society, and was to inspire the 'amour courtois' of the Western Christian Middle Ages. (See Plates 9 and 10.)

This conception of romantic love penetrated all levels of society as much through love stories as through philosophical treatises. One of the most popular of such stories was that of *Layla and Majnun* which, through the centuries, inspired the literature of the Arabic, Persian and Turkish speaking world. It originated in Arabia and there are even poems attributed to its hero, Majnun, although it may be doubted if he was ever a historical person.

Perhaps the noblest and best known version of the story is the poem of the Persian poet Nizami (1141–1209). His *Layla and Majnun*, composed in 1188, is one of the five poems which form Nizami's celebrated *Khamsa* or *Quintet*.

The poem recounts the hapless love of Qais, son of a shaikh of the tribe of the Banu'Amir, for Layla, daughter of the shaikh of a neighbouring tribe. The pair had fallen in love as schoolfellows; and so intense were the feelings of Qais that he became known to all by the name of *Majnun*, the *Possessed*; but Layla's father had refused to sanction the marriage. Forbidden the company of his beloved, Majnun became sick; and, hoping that Allah would cure his son, the father took him on a pilgrimage to the Ka'ba at Mecca, but all to no avail. Then Majnun was befriended by Naufal, an Arab chieftain who espoused his cause and went out with his followers to secure Layla by force. Twice Naufal engaged in battle with Layla's tribe; but just when victory seemed to be near, Majnun began to pray for the victory of his enemies, so great, he declared, was his love for Layla. Still the father refused to surrender his daughter and regretfully Naufal withdrew his tribesmen from the contest.

Majnun, in his despair, now sought solace in the desert where the wild animals, taking pity on the forlorn lover, became his sole companions. There he heard that Layla had been persuaded by her family to marry Ibn Salam, a merchant of Baghdad who had long sought her hand. Bitterly he complained of her broken faith. But a message came from Layla that in spite of her marriage, she still remained and always would remain faithful to their love. At last she contrived a meeting with her lover in a wood, but the encounter remained purely platonic because Layla, in spite of her great love, did not wish to be unfaithful to her lawful husband. And so once again the lovers were separated.

Time passed and Ibn Salam died, his marriage unfulfilled; and Layla, according to custom, retired from the world. Now at last it seemed that fate would allow the union of the lovers. A faithful friend led Majnun to Layla's bower and the lovers fell into a rapturous embrace. Then Majnun left her and Layla became sick. Dying, she bade her mother tell Majnun when he should visit her tomb, that she died faithful to their love and in the one hope of seeing her beloved again. When Majnun heard the news, he hastened to her graveside where for many days he wept and then died. The lovers were buried side by side. Nizami closes his poem with the dream which was vouchsafed to Majnun's faithful companion, Zayd, in which he saw the lovers wandering hand in hand in the gardens of Paradise.

The story of Layla and Majnun was frequently illustrated in Persia, Turkey and India from the fifteenth century onwards. Above all, it was Nizami's version which captured the imagination of painters. It must be remembered that these were book illustrations made for the delectation of princely or wealthy patrons. Dramatic expression would not appear to have been the preoccupation of the miniaturists of Persia and India, as it was with western painters of the same period. They show little or no concern with the focusing of attention on the emotive forces at work in their subjects. Rather at best they succeed in evoking a generalized mood which they achieve by the accumulation of detail. The end result is a harmonious blending of colour and line and its success is measured by the extent to which it pleases the eye.

Majnun Brought in Chains to Layla's Tent depicts an incident when, in order to visit his beloved, Majnun disguised himself as a beggar and had himself thus led by an old beggar woman to Layla's tent.

This beautiful painting of a desert encampment with its brilliant colours and charming genre scenes evokes an atmosphere of romantic fantasy. Majnun led in chains stands before the tent of Layla. A dog barks and small boys throw stones at him. Some women are preparing a meal; one woman sews; a herdsman milks his sheep while another plays the flute. The white tents are provided with gorgeous hangings.

R. H. Pinder-Wilson

Fig. 11a. *Layla and Majnun at School. School of Bihzad. Herat, Persia. ca. 1493.*

which the artist has illustrated here is when Layla was brought to Majnun in the desert by a hermit, but shrank from the encounter when she recollected her marriage vows. The miniature shows clearly the difference in intention between the Persian and the Indian painter. The Indian artist strives after an effect of naturalism, particularly in his treatment of landscape where he attempts to indicate recession by the tiny trees on the horizon and the distant buildings drawn in an appropriately small scale. He must have had the same aim in mind when he placed his protagonists in the middle ground. He has achieved a singularly beautiful scene in which landscape and human gesture combine in underlining the poignancy of the situation.

R.H.P-W.

Fig. 11b. *A Hermit brings Layla to the place appointed for her meeting with Majnun. Mughal School, India. ca. 1600–1610.*

Bibliography

R. H. Pinder-Wilson
Persian Painting of the Fifteenth Century
Faber and Faber, London. 1958

W. G. Archer
Indian Miniatures
New York Graphic Society, Greenwich, Connecticut. 1960

André Godard and Basil Gray
Iran; Persian Miniatures
UNESCO World Art Series
New York Graphic Society, Greenwich, Connecticut. 1956

Rubens and his First Wife in the Honeysuckle Arbour 12

Oil painting by Rubens. Flanders (now Belgium). c. 1610

For a note on Peter Paul Rubens. see *Man through his Art*, Vol. 1, *War and Peace*, Plate 14.

The finest of these woodcuts were after drawings by Bernard Solomon and are contained in the Lyon edition of 1546 and were later embodied in the Spanish and Italian translations.

The honeysuckle as a symbol of love can be traced in medieval poetry from the twelfth century. In Shakespeare's *Midsummer Night's Dream*, Oberon describes Titania's resting place:

'I know a bank where the wild thyme blows,
Where oxlips and the nodding violet grows,
Quite over-canopied with luscious woodbine (honeysuckle),
With sweet musk-roses, and with eglantine:
There sleeps Titania sometime of the night,
Lull'd in these flowers with dance and delight;'

And Titania puts her love, Bottom, to sleep with the words:

'Sleep thou, and I will wind thee in my arms.
Fairies, be gone and be all ways away.
So doth the woodbine the sweet honeysuckle
Gently entwist; the female ivy so
Enrings the barky fingers of the elm.

THIS PAINTING representing Rubens and his first wife, Isabella, in a honeysuckle arbour seems to be unique if we consider the composition within the tradition of portraiture. We may regard it as a self-portrait, a group portrait or, finally, as a portrait in the open air; while the painting unites all these characteristics, it is more novel in regard to each one of them than is usually pointed out.

Earlier full-length self-portraits are extremely rare; none of them anticipates the manner in which Rubens has shown himself with his wife in such a way that nothing betrays the fact that he is a painter and not an ordinary man. Rubens' painting, or the character of the painting, is autobiographical and intimately personal. The uninhibited freedom, so characteristic of the great Flemish painter, was only possible within the development of European art after about the year 1600.

Viewed as a group portrait, the painting is no less unusual. Earlier painters had depicted married couples in a more formal manner; never before had a man been depicted leaning over in so comfortable an attitude, nor had a woman been shown in such a relaxed posture. No earlier group portrait had so successfully merged two such contrasting poses.

Finally, the portrait in the open air ceases to be a rarity only in the seventeenth century. Even in the previous century the landscape had been the foil, or background, rather than the real environment. All this changed, however, in the seventeenth century, when a new sentiment of nature, sometimes anticipating the mood of Rousseau, is reflected in paintings of parks and landscapes; but Rubens' *Honeysuckle Arbour* precedes them. It seems to have blazed a trail; at least earlier portrait art does not appear to have provided Rubens with a model. We search in vain for prototypes in portraiture, and the question arises whether Rubens' masterpiece may not be connected with a quite different theme, and whether the painting may not have to be explained as a merging of portraiture with the representation of lovers in a landscape.

His other type of representation is known from the time of the *Carmina Burana* in the early thirteenth century and is encountered in all artistic media. Within the large variety of this group, two main types may be discerned: that in which the couples are shown standing, and that in which they are seated; there are also intermediary types between

Fig. 12a. *April. Miniature from The Book of Hours of Charles d'Angoulême ms., France, 1459–1496.*

these two. The Cleveland engagement painting of *The Two Lovers* (Plate 9) may stand for the first of these types – it is a kind of open-air counterpart to Jan van Eyck's *Arnolfini Marriage* (Plate 8), while the miniature depicting April from the Calendar in *The Book of Hours of Charles d'Angoulême* (Fig. 12a) may illustrate the second type. The Cleveland painting depicts the youth and his betrothed standing close together and follows a known medieval type; in the Calendar miniature on the other hand, the two are seated side by side, holding their right hands joined together, the youth gently embracing his lady, who holds a small dog in her left arm. Other fifteenth-century paintings of lovers anticipate both the asymmetry of the figures and the girl's posture in Rubens' painting. We note features such as the garden vegetation and the representation of full-length figures that also occur again in Rubens' picture despite the long interval in time. Full-length representations of couples existed before they acquired the character of portraits; the human beings that meet as 'anonymous lovers' in the thirteenth-century *Carmina Burana* become 'persons' in the individualizing art of the fifteenth century. Thus the theme had moved close to the portraits of individuals, but it was left to Rubens to reinforce this particular portrait quality. The master of the Cleveland painting (Plate 9) had placed his couple on a flower-studded lawn with shrubs in the background; the painter of the *April* miniature placed his couple on a grass bank with a flowery meadow under their feet and a trellis above them.

The recurrence of these features in the *Honeysuckle Arbour* makes it clear that Rubens wanted to convey more than a momentary episode in his garden. His painting must not be understood as a spontaneous and entirely personal invention designed to perpetuate a beautiful moment in open air surroundings well-known to him: rather did he take up an old tradition and recall pictorial types that depicted the quintessence of bridal happiness by showing the couple seated on a grassy bank in front of flowering vegetation. It is the union of the two right hands that proves without a doubt that this is the meaning of Rubens' painting. This union of hands appears particularly intimate and indissoluable because otherwise the two persons are but loosely connected, looking straight ahead instead of at one another. Rubens has moved to the centre of his composition this gesture of loyalty which is part of the marriage ceremonial, a sign of understanding between lovers that regularly occurs in art since classical antiquity, and which is seen, for example, in the *April* scene (Fig. 12a) and the *Arnolfini Marriage* (Plate 8). Indeed, the holding of hands had become a well-known and generally understood formula, so that Andreas Alciatus employed it in his *Emblemata* (Fig. 12b), that famous collection of symbols and allegories representing all sorts of ideas and concepts. From 1521–1531, this work achieved a large circulation in Europe. The *Emblemata* furnished the link between the betrothal pictures of the fifteenth century and the *Honeysuckle Arbour* of Rubens. The representations which interest us in this connection are those introducing the emblems for matrimony and illustrating the term 'in fidem uxoriam' (the concept of matrimonial loyalty) in the Lyon edition of Alciatus of 1546 (see note). The woodcut illustrating marriage and matrimonial loyalty preserves the iconography of the seated couple, adding, however, certain features derived from Italian Renaissance art and leading us closer to the repertoire of the age of Rubens. In the background of the woodcut, to the right, we see some buildings, while the foreground is occupied mainly by the couple seated on a grassy bank beneath an apple tree, the apple being an attribute of Venus; a small dog, a symbol of faithfulness, lies on the hem of the woman's skirt, while the man and wife hold each other by the right hand.

Rubens may have recalled this particular woodcut or some other

12. RUBENS AND HIS FIRST WIFE
IN THE HONEYSUCKLE ARBOUR
Alta Pinakothek, Munich

Rubens, *ca.* 1610.
Oil on canvas. 68½ × 52 in. : 174 × 132 cm.

During the sixteenth and seventeenth centuries, books of Emblems, especially that of Andreas Alciatus, greatly encouraged a predilection for representing scenes from legend and mythology in such a way that the episode, like hieroglyphics (as they were then understood), concealed the more general significance. A painting of this kind has a twofold meaning: it is on the one hand the image of the event depicted and may be understood as such; on the other hand, like an allegory, it points to an idea that transcends the episode. Rubens was a humanist and an erudite interpreter of archaeological themes. To be fully intelligible his *Honeysuckle Arbour* has to be interpreted in the 'Emblematic' spirit of his time.

What is so new about his image of love is the fact that its symbolism is here embodied in the two living persons portrayed. By merging symbol and portrait – and even self-portrait – the impersonal remoteness of the first is infused with life; a pictorial formula that has been permeated with personal experience. The painter has appropriated an iconographic model to portray his own life. Conversely, however, the individuals represented partake of a higher order; Rubens and his wife appear with the symbolic attributes of conjugal love.

Rubens' achievement resides in his ability to merge and reconcile different themes of art, to grasp beyond traditional symbols the basic human relationships and attitudes in the very fullness of life. An eminent student of Rubens has rightly called the *Honeysuckle Arbour* the simple embodiment of marital happiness.

Hans Kauffmann

Bibliography

Jacob Burckhardt
Rubens
Phaidon Press, London, 1950

A somewhat longer and more fully documented version of the present article appeared in *Form und Inhalt; Festschrift für O. Schmitt*, Stuttgart, 1950

13. THE BRIDAL COUPLE
Rijksmuseum, Amsterdam

Rembrandt, ca. 1666.

Oil painting. 47⅞ × 65½ in. : 121.5 × 166.5 cm

The Bridal Couple 13

Oil Painting by Rembrandt, Holland. c. 1666

The title of *Jewish Bride* was attached to the picture about 1825 while it belonged to the Vaillant Collection in Amsterdam. Since that time countless suggestions have been offered to explain the meaning of the representation, most interpretations assuming a Biblical source.

If Rembrandt intended to represent a bridal pair in Biblical disguise, this was not without precedent in contemporary Dutch art. Accordingly the figures have been variously identified as Ruth and Boaz, Esther and Ahasuerus, Tobias and Sarah, or Isaac and Rebecca. Who, then, might be the Biblical characters to whom Rembrandt alluded here, with the consent of his patrons? It now seems certain that Rembrandt followed, with some variations, Raphael's composition in the Loggia of the Vatican representing *Isaac and Rebecca Spied Upon by King Abimelech*. In Rembrandt's painting this subject is no longer indicated, since Abimelech has disappeared. The two figures, moreover, are no longer seated, their costumes reflect the contemporary fashion (most obvious in the headdress), and the man's position in changed from a profile to a three-quarter view. The pair now nearly fill the picture plane in the manner of a portrait, and the spirit of the scene is transformed from an amorous to a more solemn one.

While granting some plausibility to the 'Isaac and Rebecca' theory, we cannot overlook another possibility, namely, that Rembrandt was alluding to 'Jacob and Rachel'. There is a painting of this subject by Rembrandt's contemporary, Dirck Santvoort, which shows a striking similarity in the attitude of the couple and in the gesture of the man. This picture bears no date but it is obviously earlier than Rembrandt's *The Bridal Couple*, probably about 1640. A drawing by Hugo van der Goes in Oxford had treated the same subject in a very similar arrangement. The tradition lived on in the sixteenth century as we find in Holbein's little drawing of *Jacob and Rachel* in Basle, where the gestures are even closer to those in the Rembrandt composition. It may be that Rembrandt saw Santvoort's painting or a similar representation of the Jacob and Rachel subject after he had done the drawing of Isaac and Rebecca, and that this new impression had some bearing on the final version of *The Jewish Bride*.   J.R.

THIS PICTURE of *The Bridal Couple* in Amsterdam brings us to Rembrandt's last period. This magnificent painting, dating from the early or middle sixties, reveals all the colouristic power and profound humanity of the mature Rembrandt. Rembrandt has obviously painted a bridal pair from life, but he has endowed the figures with a symbolic character as if he wished to express through this portrait the meaning of the marital relationship in general. He has suggested this meaning in profound human terms which are both emotional and spiritual, both intimate and monumental.

As in all Rembrandt's late works the figures are broadly displayed, the woman almost frontally, the man turned slightly toward her. Following the Venetian precedent they are represented in three-quarter length, within an oblong frame. They seem to float rather than to stand in a world of mysterious dimness. One gains the impression that the light comes from within the picture as much as from some outside source. It strikes the forms with conscious selection, stressing their frontality and causing the colour to flare up with unusual intensity in the woman's scarlet skirt and the man's golden olive sleeve. The inner relationship between the two figures is brought out in their postures, their facial expressions, and above all, in their gestures, which are as unusual in Dutch portraiture as they are significant. Although the sensual implications are unmistakable, the solemnity and tenderness speak to us first. There is reflected what might be called a patriarchal conception of bridal relationship in which the man becomes the responsible owner of the woman and cherishes her as his possession.

We can say with certainty that the gestures are most unusual for an ordinary Dutch portrait. This fact makes it very probable that Rembrandt intended here to represent his patrons as a Biblical pair and it was natural also for him to rely upon a tradition which would justify the symbolical treatment.

Rembrandt's subjects often show a spirit which is akin to the ideals of Puritanism. But there is still a wide gulf between the all-embracing humanity of Rembrandt and that combination of morality and outward cleanliness which many Dutch painters exhibit in their portraits. A comparison leaves no doubt that Rembrandt rose far above the pedantry, sobriety and narrowness of the average Dutch attitude of the time. His free and universal nature embraced not only daily life but the mystery of human existence as well.

The element of mystery is often enhanced in Rembrandt's portraits of his own choice, or in those in which the sitters allowed him to indulge his romantic and pictorial fancy. Such portraits are the *Man with a Magnifying Glass* and its pendant the *Woman with a Pink* (Figs. 13a and 13b), both obviously dating from Rembrandt's last period. Even greater freedom is shown in the more famous double portrait of *The Bridal Couple* of our Plate, which represents the same sitters as a bridal pair. In this picture both persons appear slightly younger. Rembrandt portrayed the man alone at an earlier date (1659) in a fine oil sketch, now in the Metropolitan Museum also. There he wears the same large hat as in *The Bridal Couple* and his mantle is thrown over his shoulder in the fashion popular in the early Louis XIV period.

Fig. 13a. *Man with a Magnifying Glass.*
Rembrandt, Holland. ca. 1662–1665.

Fig. 13b. *Lady with a Pink. Rembrandt.*

The two companion portraits mentioned (Figs. 13a and 13b) show, in their relation to each other, some deviation from the standard type of companion portraits. The woman's figure is seen almost in profile as she faces her husband, and her head is inclined in his direction. The position of the man's right hand might be interpreted as pointing to the woman in the traditional way, but its main function here is to hold a magnifying glass. Moreover, the hand is unusually inconspicuous by the absence of any highlight. The concentration on facial expression is strong. The heads emerge from the surrounding darkness with a mysterious glow and the meditative gaze of the eyes expresses extreme inner absorption. The luminous red and gold, particularly in the woman's costume and jewellery, add to the exotic romanticism of these portraits. The emotional impact, never surpassed by Rembrandt, finds adequate expression in the richness and the subtlety of the pictorial performance.

Jakob Rosenberg

Bibliography

Jakob Rosenberg
Rembrandt. 1606–1669
Phaidon Press, London, 1964

Henri Focillon and Ludwig Goldscheider
Rembrandt: *Paintings, Drawings and Etchings*
Phaidon Press, London, 1960

14. BAZ BAHADUR AND RUPMATI
Faizullah

Late seventeenth century.
Miniature painting. 10½ × 7½ in. : 26.5 × 19.2 cm.

Baz Bahadur and Rupmati 14

Miniature Painting, India. Eighteenth century

The kingdom of Malwa had once been a part of the Mughal Empire and during the reign of Baz Bahadur the young Mughal Emperor Akbar set out to regain his lost empire. When Akbar had firmly established himself on the imperial throne, he began a series of military campaigns against the various kingdoms and principalities which were once under the suzerainty of the Mughal emperor. One of the first of these campaigns was directed at the weak and ill-administered kingdom of Malwa. The imperial forces were led by a cruel and profligate commander, Adham Khan. Baz Bahadur bravely went out against the army of Adham Khan and was defeated. His capital, Sarangpur, was taken. As was the custom in India at the time, Baz Bahadur had left instructions that the women of his court, among them the beautiful and beloved Rupmati, were to be put to death if he was defeated, rather than have them fall into the hands of the enemy. In the shock and panic of defeat, Rupmati is stabbed but not killed. The other women of the court are seized by

Fig. 14a. *The Battle between Baz Bahadur and the Imperial Army and Rupmati's Suicide. Miniature from the 'Akbar-Nama', Mughal School, India. ca. 1600.*

OF THE MANY historical love-stories which have provided a subject for the painters and poets of India, one of the most famous is that of Baz Bahadur and Rupmati. In the mid-sixteenth century Baz Bahadur, a Muslim prince, ruled over the kingdom of Malwa, a region of streams, lakes and mountains in the very centre of India. The Indo-Islamic courts of India were marked by an elegance and refinement which is vividly preserved for us in the miniature paintings of the period. A poet and by all accounts a very accomplished musician and singer, Baz Bahadur took more interest in the elegant pleasures of his court than in the efficient administration of his kingdom. The great love of his life was the Hindu beauty, Rupmati. In a court famous for its beautiful women, Rupmati was considered the most beautiful. Of the songs sung about these two lovers, some are said to be those which Baz Bahadur himself composed and sang to Rupmati.

In the many paintings we have of Baz Bahadur and Rupmati, we often see them riding in the hills by moonlight or resting by mountain streams, always gazing into each other's eyes. In our Plate they ride out on a stormy night accompanied by two attendants. The moon scarcely shows itself, covered by dark clouds, and the stars shine dully in a grey sky. Against this dark background of a blue-grey sky, the brown hills and the dull silver of the moonlit water, the riders stand out boldly in their vivid colours, their brightly lit faces turned to each other. In our other illustration (Fig. 14b) they rest on a hill-top, in an exquisitely beautiful setting. They are surrounded by birds and flowering trees. In the distance is a beautiful mountain landscape, with a pair of leopards, a pool full of lotuses, a crescent moon and hundreds of bright stars.

The story of Baz Bahadur and Rupmati has a tragic end. Baz Bahadur, a brave but ill-equipped warrior, is defeated in the wars against the Mughal Empire. His capital and his palace are taken and Rupmati kills herself (see note). Baz Bahadur himself survives his defeat and regains his kingdom, only to lose it again. He spends several years wandering as an exile and finally submits himself to the imperial authority, taking office under the emperor. He is said to be buried by the side of his beloved Rupmati on a ridge in the middle of the lake at Ujjain.

This story is first related in a contemporary account, the *Akbar-Nama*, the chronicle of the Mughal emperor Akbar's reign, written by his court historian Abu Fazl. Though the book is clearly biased against Baz Bahadur, one of the most moving passages is Abu Fazl's account of Rupmati's suicide:-

'When the form of Baz Bahadur's defeat appeared in the mirror of results, those devil-born ones acted according to the arrangement (see note) and with the water of the sword wiped out some of those fairy-framed puppets from the page of life. Some were wounded and yet retained a breath of life, and for many the turn of slaughter had not come, when the victorious troops marched into the city. The villains had not time to lay hands on these innocent women. The chief of them was Rupmati, renowned throughout the world for her beauty and charm. Baz Bahadur was deeply attached to her and used to pour out his heart in Hindi poems descriptive of his love. A monster who had been left in

Fig. 14b. *Baz Bahadur and Rupmati resting in the hills while on a moonlight ride.*
Garwhal School, India. ca. 18th century.

Fig. 14c. *Rupmati's Suicide (detail from Fig. 14a.)*

Adham Khan's men. The general sends for the famous beauty, but Rupmati poisons herself rather than give herself up to him.

The painting of Baz Bahadur and Rupmati, illustrated in our main plate, was probably executed in the province of Oudh about 1770 AD. It is in the style of Faqirullah Khan; the picture itself is signed *Faizullah*, an artist who appears to have worked in the circle of Faqirullah. The miniature is an example of the Late Mughal style.

The school of Mughal painting in India can be said to have begun in the reign of the Mughal Emperors Humayun (1530–1556) and Akbar the Great (1556–1605). Humayun was greatly impressed by the Persian tradition of miniature painting, which he saw during his exile in Persia. When he returned to Delhi as Emperor, he brought with him two Persian masters, Mir Sayyid Ali (see Plate 11) and Abd us-Samad, from the court of Shah Tahmasp I. Under Humayun's son Akbar these painters trained a large studio of Indo-Muslim and Hindu artists who initiated the Mughal School of painting; an Indo-Islamic style, incorporating several distinctively indigenous traditions, it flourished under Akbar and his successors, Jahangir (1605–1627) and Shahjahan (1628–1658), the builder of the Taj Mahal. With the accession of the Emperor Aurangzeb (1658–1707) and the strict religious orthodoxy of his reign, which discouraged figural art, the imperial patronage declined. The painters sought provincial patrons, as in the present example, and though there was a revival of interest in the arts at the Imperial court, the tradition and the impetus had now been dispersed. As we see here, the style continued through the eighteenth century, and even into the nineteenth.

charge of her lifted his sword and inflicted several severe wounds on her. Just then the victorious army arrived and saved the half-slaughtered beauty…but Rupmati, her faithful blood aglow from her love for Baz Bahadur, bravely drank a cup of deadly poison and carried her honour to the hidden chambers of annihilation.'*

The story has in it all the elements of a classic romance, the poet-prince, the beautiful lady, the cruel enemy, the mountain kingdom with its lakes and streams and its moonlit nights, the poet's defeat and exile, the lady's tragic end, the final reunion in death. It is not surprising then that this story has been so often celebrated in paintings and poems.

The Editors

Bibliography

J. U. S. Wilkinson
Mughal Painting
Faber and Faber, London, 1948

Douglas Barrett and Basil Gray
Indian Painting
Skira

W. G. Archer
Indian Miniatures
New York Graphic Society, Greenwich, Connecticut. 1960

* After the trans. by H. Beveridge.

15 Radha and Krishna in the Forest of Brindhaban

Miniature painting, Kangra School, India. Eighteenth century

PERHAPS IN NO OTHER manifestation do we see the two-fold nature of the Indian mind as clearly as in the Krishna story. This dichotomy runs through all Indian art and literature: the metaphysical religious aspect and the joyful pagan revelling in earthly sensual beauty – the 'romantic sensuality and loving innocence which is perhaps the chief Indian contribution to cultured living'. In the Krishna legend these two aspects are brought together, giving us one of the most extraordinary manifestations of a whole culture. Radha and Krishna, the ideal lovers, are the theme of much literature, poetry, song, painting and festival. The spontaneous joy and sensuous delight which pervades their art belies the image of the Indian people as a mournful, poverty-stricken one. For the story of Krishna, the adored lover, belongs to no elite, but to everyone, and has influenced the Indian belief that passionate love is a symbol of God. For Krishna is both lover and God. If the search for God is the great purpose of life, then the great experience that comes nearest to it is the ecstasy of love.

The cult of Krishna, of Krishna the lover, began to grow in importance from the tenth century onwards, although the first mention of Krishna is in the sixth century BC. In the ninth or tenth century AD his story is developed in the *Bhagavata Purana*. The Krishna story falls into two parts. The first is concerned with the early years of his life, when he is brought up among cowherds in order to escape assassination by the ruling tyrant; the second deals with his later life as a model prince. This (with the exception of the episode of the Battle of the Mahabharata – see *Man through his Art*, Vol. 1, *War and Peace*, Plate 8 – where he propounds the famous *Bhagavat-Gita* or *The Song of God*) is, in contrast to the first part, dull and conventional and, consequently Krishna, the model prince, is largely forgotten.

Krishna the cowherd, spontaneous, free and enchanting to all eyes, was, of course, the hero to appeal to a people for whom romantic love was a response to a deep part of their nature. This feeling for romantic love has manifested itself in Indian culture from the earliest times, whereas in other cultures such feelings were regarded with suspicion. In India, the physical beauty of the beloved and the raptures of love were looked upon as noble, tender and profound. It presumes the perfect concord between the souls of the lovers. This, in fact, is sacred love, for when mind and body are engrossed in another this 'joyous state of selflessness is very near to divine love'. As Coomaraswamy says:

'In the absolute self-surrender of the human soul in Radha to the divine in Krishna is summed up all love . . . .
there is no place for the distinction, always foreign to Indian thought, of sacred and profane'.

The background to the paintings in Plates 14 and 15 is the love poetry of Indian literature. There are, however, three great poems which deal with the story of Radha and Krishna, namely, *The Gita Govinda* of Jayadeva (twelfth century), *The Love Songs* of Vidyapati (ca. 1352) and *The Rasikapriya* of Keshav Das (1580–1601). Kangra painting is mainly the visual expression of the *Rasikapriya* of Keshav Das and the conceptions of Nayaka, the Lover, and Nayika, the Beloved, were clearly formulated by him. In fact, a few titles of some of the innumer-

Under the enlightened patronage of two rulers in the Punjab Hill States – Raja Govarbhan Chand (1744–1773), ruler of Guler, and Sansar Chand II (1775–1823) of Kangra – artists who had fled the disturbed courts of Northern India found refuge and the school of Kangra painting was born. It was Dr. A. K. Coomaraswamy who first brought the Kangra School to the public's attention. As he describes it, 'Rarely has any other art combined so little fear with so much tenderness, so much delight with such complete renunciation. If the Chinese have taught us best how to understand the life of Nature manifest in water and in mountains, Indian art at least can teach us how not to misunderstand desire, for we are constantly reminded here that the soul of sweet delight can never be defiled.'

Until the early centuries AD, Krishna had been vaguely identified with the second member of the Hindu Trinity, Vishnu. In the sixth century, however, two books – the *Harivansa* (or *Genealogy of Krishna*) and the *Vishnu Purana* – related his story and this was repeated in greater detail in a book of the ninth or tenth century, the *Bhagavata Purana*. According to this text, Vishnu as loving preserver watched the struggle between gods and demons and the efforts of the wicked to discomfort the good. When the forces of evil appeared to triumph, he entered the world, slew demons and corrected the balance. He had intervened in this way on nine previous occasions and it was on the plea of Earth herself that he again took flesh and appeared as Krishna. His immediate goal was to slay a particular tyrant – a demon in human form – and thus encourage the good. For this purpose he was born into a princely family in the city of Mathura in northern India. Fearing the birth of his destroyer, the tyrant king had imprisoned Krishna's parents. To avoid the child's destruction they handed Krishna over to a family of wealthy cowherds. He was brought up in the forest of Brindhaban, taught to graze cattle, play the flute and in general to live the life of a cowherd boy. During this time he warded off attacks from roving demons, aided the cowherds by the occasional exercise of supernatural powers and delighted both boys and girls and men and women by his strong magnetic charm. Among the younger women Krishna had a special favourite but the

15. RADHA AND KRISHNA IN THE
FOREST OF BRINDHABAN
Knagra School, India

18th Century.
Miniature painting. Approx. actual size.

Fig. 15c. *Radha and Krishna in a Grove. Kangra School, India. 18th century.*

As I chained the dark one (Krishna),
I felt a river flooding in my heart
I devoured that liquid face
I felt stars shooting around me.'

and

'The trees grow again. Fresh flowers bloom.
The Spring comes with the fragrant Southern wind and bees are drunk.
The forest of Brindhaban is filled with new airs.
Krishna has come.
On the river bank, adorned with groves,
New lovers are lost in love.
Intoxicated by the honey of Mango blossoms,
Kokila (birds) freshly sing.
The hearts of young girls are drunken with delight.
The forest is charged with a new flavour of love . . . .'

The Kangra artist's delight in nature, which is used as the lyrical expression of love, is depicted in this painting with radiant charm. Every motif is an expression of lyrical ecstasy. The creepers twined round the trunks of the trees, the birds in pairs, the abundance of flowers, the bed of leaves, the swiftly flowing stream, and the luxuriant feeling of the whole painting have a sensual and innocent grace.

Anil de Silva

established conventions and authority. The lover puts love above everything. The prince demonstrates Vishnu's power; the cowherd Vishnu's love.

William Archer

Bibliography

Translated by Deben Battacharya, Introduction by W. G. Archer
Love Songs of Vidyapati
George Allen and Unwin, London, 1963

Dr. M. S. Randhawa
Kangra Paintings on Love
National Museum, New Delhi, 1962

Jayadeva (trans. & illust. by G. Keyt)
Gita Govinda
Kutub Publishers, Bombay, 1947

Fig. 15d. *A Wedding Scene. Rajasthani or Malwa School (?), India. ca. 1700.*

16 ROBERT ANDREWS AND HIS WIFE   Gainsborough, *ca.* 1748
National Gallery, London   Oil painting. 27½ × 47 in. : 69.8 × 119 cm.

Robert Andrews and his Wife 16

Oil painting by Gainsborough, England. c. 1748

Thomas Gainsborough was born in Suffolk in 1727. He was sent to London about the year 1740 to study and work under a French painter and engraver. He married in London and returned to Suffolk some time after 1746. He moved to Ipswich in 1752 and then to Bath where, his reputation established, he was greatly in demand as a portrait painter. He lived in Bath for several years and finally returned to London in 1774, where he lived until his death in 1788. He exhibited regularly at the Royal Academy until a quarrel with the Academy in 1784. In his later years he was greatly in demand at the Court Gainsborough was very much the natural, indigenous genius when compared with his intellectual, academic rival Sir Joshua Reynolds. Like Reynolds, Gainsborough was a portraitist by profession, in response to the demands of the time, though he had a natural preference for painting landscape, a preference he had little time or encouragement to develop. Yet in the several landscape sketches he made and in the landscape backgrounds to some of his portraits, as in this picture of *Robert Andrews and his Wife*, Gainsborough establishes himself as one of the first masters of the English landscape and a precursor of Constable.

THIS EARLY MASTERPIECE by Gainsborough can be enjoyed for its deliciously fresh and exciting handling of paint, as a wonderful piece of naturalistic painting, or as an idyll of the English countryside in late summer. It is all these things, and extraordinarily precocious for its date. But it is a picture which also has a quite specific social significance. Robert Andrews, of Auberies, near Bulmer in Essex, was married to Frances Mary, daughter of Mr. and Mrs. William Carter of Ballingdon House, Sudbury, in 1748. He was then twenty-two, she about eighteen. Gainsborough's canvas was evidently a marriage portrait – certainly, on stylistic grounds, it cannot have been painted very much later than 1748 – and it shows Robert, a little too well-dressed really to be going out shooting, standing in an elegant but informal pose, gun under arm, with his young bride seated demurely beside him, dressed in her very best bonnet and gown. To the right a cornfield is included in the scene, the corn already cut and neatly stooked. In the fields beyond, a flock of sheep is quietly grazing. Neither the Andrews not the Carters were gentry of sufficient importance to be mentioned in the county histories, but they had status, and the young couple are depicted here as master and mistress of their estate, presiding over the tangible evidence of their income and standing in the county-land.

Landed wealth was what every girl and every parent of a marriageable daughter looked for in a husband. For marriage in the eighteenth century, in England, was principally a matter of alliance – the two words seem almost to have been synonymous. Parents of both boys and girls began considering and writing to the families of suitable partners for their offspring almost as soon as the latter had reached their 'teens. Friends and relatives were ready ambassadors and pursued the interests of their cause with all the relish which went into the fixing of a Court job or any other intrigue. Much hard bargaining went on before dowry was matched against settlement, and before the marriage contract, that ever-popular source of comic situation in contemporary farce and opera, was eventually signed. It was not unusual, in the earlier part of the century as in the seventeenth, for the parents to conclude negotiations without so much as consulting the two young people whose life's happiness they were thus disposing.

For the girl, married life was always hard. In both Defoe and Fielding we find a wife regarded as very much an upper servant. She was expected not only to run the household and supervise the servants, but to manage the farm and brewhouse, make what clothes were needed, and entertain anyone her husband might bring in. She shared little of her husband's life, and certainly nothing of its public side; she did not even hunt as yet. She was expected to be unobtrusive, quiet and obedient; to remember Squire Western's maxim that women should come in with the first dish at dinner, and go out with the first glass. She probably bore a child most years and saw many of these little mites die of smallpox or other now preventable diseases before they had reached the age of five or six. Thomas Gray was the sole survivor of twelve children and this was not uncommon. Visiting and gossip provided the lighter side of a life which was plentifully filled with work and sorrow.

Merchants' wives were always the most emancipated, and with the proliferation of Assembly rooms, of balls and parties and entertainments of all kinds, in short with the establishment of Society in the county towns, the importance of women naturally increased. With new opportunities for mixing freely (within one's class), the proportion of love matches also tended to increase. There were many cases of forcible abductions and celebrated elopements. Before Lord Hardwicke's Marriage Act, which from 1754 enforced the publication of banns, the production of a licence and a ceremony in a church or public chapel, the actual solemnisation of matrimony was only too easily performed. The vicinity of the Fleet prison became notorious for the celebration of marriages by dissolute parsons. Signs were hung out, 'marriages performed within', and touts attempted to entice the passers-by inside. Rather more fashionable was Alexander Keith, who performed like services more agreeably (and expensively) in the West End. Gainsborough was married secretly at Mr. Keith's little chapel in Mayfair in 1746, and thither, after the briefest acquaintance, the Duke of Hamilton whisked the beautiful Elizabeth Gunning at half-past twelve one February night. To make a dazzling exception to the rule that the portionless girl, however talented and pretty, was likely to remain a spinster for the rest of her days, the penniless Miss Gunning married two dukes, refused a third, and was mother to four more.

The eighteenth century was obviously far from unromantic, and it was much too close to the earth and too well acquainted with death to be in the least inhibited in the way it took its pleasures. Side by side with the drinking and gaming on an excessive scale went a taste for rakishness, indulged with characteristic gusto. But, however dissolute the life of the capital and however many clandestine marriages were celebrated in the precincts of the Fleet (some two or three thousand a year), when all is said and done it is Gainsborough's canvas which gives us the truer picture of eighteenth century life. Nine tenths of the population lived outside London and few towns (Bristol was the main exception) boasted more than thirty or forty thousand inhabitants. England was predominantly rural well into the time spoken of as the 'Industrial Revolution', and the values of the squirearchy ruled the shires. Evidence for the poorer classes is largely lacking, but there is little reason to suppose that, as with the gentry, the yeomen and the farmers, marriage was normally anything but a most practical affair all the way down the social scale.

John Hayes

Bibliography

Mary Woodall
Thomas Gainsborough: his life and work
British Painters Series, Phoenix House,
London, 1949

Mary Woodall
The Letters of Thomas Gainsborough
New York Graphic Society, Greenwich,
Connecticut, 1963

Fig. 16a. *The Marriage Proposal.*
From 'Marriage à la Mode',
by Hogarth, England. 1744.

鈴木春信画

17. THE LOVERS IN THE SNOW
British Museum, London

Suzuki Harunobu, 1766-1768.
Coloured woodcut.   10½ × 7¾ in. : 26.6 × 19.9 cm.

The Lovers in the Snow 17

Japanese coloured wood-cut by Suzuki Harunobu. 1766–1768

The manufacture of paper, printing, printed books and even the use of movable type were all inventions known to the Chinese, the Japanese and the Koreans before they were known in any other part of the world. The oldest extant printed book is an illustrated Chinese religious text of the ninth century AD found at Tun Huang in northwest China. Early printing in Japan dates at least from the late Nara (seventh to eighth centuries AD) or the early Heian (eighth to twelfth centuries AD) periods. The commonest technique involved the use of wooden blocks or wooden 'type'. Printing seems to have flourished in the Kamakura period (twelfth to fourteenth centuries AD) and there are several examples of Buddhist icons, fans, handscrolls and even armour with printed designs. The religious icons were a cheap and popular art form and rooms and doorways often had printed images of protective deities placed in them. The handscrolls and fans, with printed reproductions of paintings and designs, were limited to an exclusive upper-class

IN THIS WOOD-CUT by the Japanese master Suzuki Harunobu we have one of the most exquisite pictorial expressions of love, of the grace and harmony of a relationship between a man and a woman. The two lovers, one in a dominant black and the other in a subtle, broken white, stand out soft and warm in a winter-bared landscape, whose harshness is presented to us in a single statement, a row of sharp and jagged branches covered in frost. The flowing lines of their long robes converge and their delicate, stylised faces are gently inclined towards each other. Under a protective umbrella they stand together, 'The Crow and the Heron' – the picture's subtitle – traditional opposites, in black and white, reminding us of the classic Chinese *yin-yang*, the dual principles of light and dark, of heat and cold, of male and female. The umbrella itself is partly obliterated in a scarcely noticeable covering of snow, which blends with the background. For the rest there are only large areas of white, an expanse of snow. Undoubtedly one of Harunobu's masterpieces, the whole picture is worked out in varying tones of white with a single central area of black. The grace and elegance associated with this early master of the wood-cut is crystallised in this work, a picture at once so simple and perfect.

The exceptional and permanent quality of the best Japanese art is the economy which it employs with an assurance and precision unlike anything seen outside the cultures of the Far East. It is this economy

Fig. 17a. *Two Lovers. Okumura Masanobu, Japan. 1685–1764.*

Fig. 17b. *Lovers by a Lake. Ando Hiroshige, Japan. 1797–1858.*

audience. From about the fifteenth century onwards there were numerous picture-books and collections of *haiku* poetry, erotic albums and books of moral guidance for women, all with printed illustration. Though Kamakura printing had in it the elements of successful colour-printing, the colours were usually applied to the print by hand. True colour printing was essentially a development of the Tokugawa period (seventeenth to nineteenth centuries AD). The earliest books with printed illustrations in colour were mathematical and scientific texts of the mid-seventeenth century. This long tradition of printing saw its culmination in the printed wood-cuts of the *Ukiyoe* school (see text). Up to that time printed illustrations had been mostly ingenious reproductions of already existing paintings or designs. With Hishikawa Moronubu's illustrations of 1568, we have the first real woodblock prints which were 'works of art in their own right' with their own rules of form appropriate to the medium'.

Just as the woodblock technique of the *Ukiyoe* prints was little different from the traditional methods of printing, the *Ukiyoe* style itself drew upon the various traditions of Japanese art, both secular and religious, popular and aristocratic, indigenous and foreign. The early *Ukiyoe* prints were in black-and-white and then in a two- or three-colour technique. Harunobu is traditionally credited with the development of the polychrome print, with several colours. His work is known from the early 1760's, but it was not until about 1765 that he produced prints in several colours. A subtle and delicate colourist, the new medium was exactly suited to his genius. He understood at once the true nature of the medium. His prints were conceived as a colouristic whole, with no distinction between the drawing and the colour. In the short space of five years between 1765 and his death in 1770 he produced nearly seven hundred printed sheets. Essentially a master of the wood-cut, he produced little else other than these prints, some erotica and illustrated books and a few paintings.

Less than a hundred years later, with the death of Ando Hiroshige (see Fig. 17b) in 1858, the great tradition of the woodblock print, by which Japanese art is best known to the West, came to an end.†

Bibliography

D. B. Waterhouse
Harunobu and his age
British Museum, London, 1964

J. Hillier
Japanese Colour Prints
Phaidon Press, London, 1957

above all which distinguishes between the beautiful and the pretty. It is the style of a high civilization intensely concerned with the beautiful, and it is this essential beauty of a human experience which is distilled here in the subtle juxtaposition of warmth and cold, of black and white. In Japanese painting, as in Japanese poetry and drama, a single line, phrase or gesture is often used to convey a whole atmosphere, to define an entire relationship. We are told very little about these lovers, who look alike and even dress alike. We cannot identify them as we do van Eyck's Arnolfini or Grant Wood's American farmers (see Plates 8 and 20), but we know the one important thing about them: that they are lovers, that they have between them an ecstatic but highly-controlled relationship. We see nothing of the garden they stand in, but we know that it is winter. It is a single, though by no means simple, theme rendered at its purest and highest pitch.

Sēnake Bandaranayake

The *Ukiyoe* paintings of Japan, of which the wood-cut was the most characteristic medium, were an urban, secular art, by their very definition given to representing 'the fleeting, passing world' (*Ukiyoe* being a Japanese Buddhist term meaning 'the sad, transitory world'). Confined almost exclusively to a gay, colourful world of love, of beautiful courtesans, of the theatre and the tea-houses, of the gayer districts of a metropolis at work and play, *Ukiyoe* was a comparatively modern development satisfying the need for a popular, middle-class art. The development of the woodcut and the polychrome print in the sixteenth and seventeenth centuries (see note) made cheap and wide-scale distribution possible, so that the *Ukiyoe* prints, such as our present picture, were in a way a sort of highly civilised pin-up.

The grace and refinement of Harunobu's style reveal his 'leanings towards a vanished, courtly age' such as the Heian period (794–1185 AD) perpetuated in great novels like the *Tale of Genji**. The world of the Heian court had seen a lively relationship between men and women; women then enjoyed a vigorous independence, the authors of the two great prose works the *Tale of Genji* and the *Pillow Book* both being women. In the civil wars which followed, women gradually lost their independence and by the Tokugawa or Edo period (seventeenth to nineteenth century) it was only among the courtesans and in the tea-houses and other places of entertainment in the Yoshiwara district of Tokyo that women of spirit and independence could easily be found. The Yoshiwara was thus a favourite quarter of the *Ukiyoe* artists. Harunobu's models were often courtesans from the Yoshiwara but, as in this picture, he transforms them and projects them into a world of pure and ideal experience.†

* See *Man through his Art*, Vol. 2, *Music*, Plate 12.
†The second half of this text and the note are largely based on D. B. Waterhouse's *Harunobu and his age*.

18 Antoine Lavoisier and his Wife

Oil painting by Jacques-Louis David, France. 1789

THIS PICTURE portrays a marriage of rare happiness. The man, Antoine Lavoisier, was a great scientist, one of the founders of modern chemistry, and yet he is not the most important figure in the picture. Seated at the table and engaged in work, he has interrupted his writing to look up at his young wife. She stands close to him, leaning slightly forward, her left hand on his shoulder. The attitude of both reflects the close union between the couple which extended even to Lavoisier's work.

In 1789, the year the painting was executed, Lavoisier published his *Traité Elémentaire de Chimie*, one of those singular achievements in which the French genius seems to excel, in which he expounded the new science with lucidity and cogency. The second volume of this work described Lavoisier's experiments as well as the instruments invented by him to carry them out. It was illustrated by thirteen plates designed and engraved by Madame Lavoisier. Some of these instruments appear on the table. A portfolio resting on the chair to the left may allude to her drawings, just as the text on which Lavoisier is working may be the manuscript of his celebrated book.

The painter of this double portrait, Jacques-Louis David, was one of the masters of the French Neo-Classical style round 1800. A revolutionary, like the period in which he lived, he replaced the softly blending tones of the late Baroque with cool, contrasting colours and clear, vigorous outlines. His portrait of Lavoisier is dominated by the white and black of the couple and the crimson red of the table cloth. This red may be a little too crimson and there may be too much of it, but it introduces into the painting something like a fanfare of glory. Without it, the couple posed against the beautifully subdued bluish background might present no more than an intimate family scene, but the red conveys something of the importance of the scientific work which had just come into existence.

It seems that in depicting the couple David deliberately alluded to a traditional theme, frequently represented in ancient art and a favourite of the great French classical painter, Poussin, whom David particularly admired; this theme, 'The Poet and his Muse' or 'The Philosopher and his Muse', occurs, for instance, on a Roman sarcophagus (see Fig. 18a) of the second century AD (now in the Louvre), discovered early in the eighteenth century in Rome where David may well have seen it. With this learned and delightful allusion the painter may well have responded to Lavoisier's wish that he convey in the painting the importance of his young wife – whom Lavoisier's biographer has called 'le charme de sa vie' – in his life and his work. In any event, the portrait is recognized as one of David's masterpieces.

Lavoisier's tragic end casts a shadow over this work and its author. In 1794, at the height of the terror of the French Revolution, Lavoisier was accused, convicted on baseless charges and sentenced to death. At his trial one of his admirers had the courage to read out a paper prepared by the Academy of Sciences setting forth the importance of Lavoisier's work for the future of science. Clemency was requested for a scientist of world renown. The answer of the judges was: 'the Republic has no need of scholars'. Lavoisier himself had only asked for a few days' reprieve in order to finish his last scientific work. Even

Jacques-Louis David (1748–1825). The artist's first visit to Rome and his contact with Italian art and the works of antiquity which he found there produced a revolution in his style. The vigour and severity of his art made him one of the greatest artists of French Neo-Classicism. After his picture *Serment des Horaces*, painted for Louis XVI, he was considered by his students and by the public to be the regenerator of French painting. Unfortunately, during the Revolution David not only joined the Members of the Convention, but (as one of his biographers explains) 'dishonoured himself without understanding what he did .... the only excuse which could be given to his odious acts was that he was a dupe and an instrument in the hands of Robespierre and dipped his hands in blood.' But the terror came down on even the most fanatical revolutionaries and later on he was accused in turn, imprisoned and nearly lost his head. He owed his liberation partly to the courage of his wife. Under Napoleon the First, David was an important member of the Committee of Public Instruction, and in fact from that time onwards gave up politics. Under Louis XVIII he moved to Brussels and never returned to Paris, although he was assured of a pardon. He died in Belgium in 1825. Among his most celebrated works are *The Death of Marat* and *The Coronation of Napoleon*.

18. ANTOINE LAVOISIER AND HIS WIFE
Rockefeller Institute of Medical Research, New York

David, 1789.
Oil painting.   120 × 84 in. : 304.8 × 213 cm.

Bibliography

M. Michaud
Biographie Universelle. Volume 10
Paris, 1855

that was refused and he died under the guillotine. Jacques-Louis David, who had painted Lavoisier and his wife only five years before, was one of the most fanatical and merciless members of the Revolutionary Convention. We do not know if Madame Lavoisier, who had once been a pupil of David's, implored him to save her husband, but we do know that he undertook nothing to save a man of whose innocence and genius he must have been aware.

Otto von Simson

Fig. 18a. *The Sarcophagus of the Muses. Roman. 2nd century* AD.

19 Argenteuil

Oil painting by Edouard Manet, France. 1874

DURING THE SUMMER of 1874, Manet frequently went to Argenteuil, a suburb of Paris and a popular rendezvous for boating on the river Seine. Caillebotte, a rich young painter, had a house there to which he welcomed Manet, his friend and master.

Manet worked at Argenteuil on a few of the rare paintings of his which were truly Impressionist. It was during the last ten years of his life that Manet was attracted by landscape, for until then he had preferred interiors and portraits.

The couple in this picture are a typical example of robust, youthful holiday-makers taking time off from work, at a sunny riverside or seaside resort. Though there is nothing here to indicate the exact relationship between them, the situation – where a young man and a young woman spend a summer day walking by the river, boating, as they are doing here, or picnicking – is one so relevant to our theme and as familiar to us today as it must have been to the painter, who recorded it so freshly and vividly nearly a hundred years ago.

This couple in the boat are in complete harmony with the landscape. Manet never made an abstraction of the human figure; it always had an important place in his outdoor scenes. The man and woman

Edouard Manet was born in Paris on the 25th of January, 1832 and died there on the 30th of April, 1883. One of the most outstanding figures of French nineteenth century art and a most controversial painter in his time, he caused a great scandal by the frank nakedness of the women in two of his masterpieces, *Déjeuner sur l'Herbe* and *Olympia*, painted after Giorgione's *Concert Champêtre* (see *Man through his Art*, Vol. 2, *Music*, Plate 9) and Titian's *Venus*. Though not an Impressionist himself, Manet was one of the central figures in the group of painters who brought about that major development in the history of European painting. He worked with the great Impressionist painter Monet and with Renoir at Argenteuil and, though he did not adopt the characteristic techniques of Impressionism, he was undoubtedly much affected by it; under

Fig. 19a. *Chez le Père Lathuile. Edouard Manet, France. 1879.*

19. ARGENTEUIL
Musée des Beaux Arts, Tournai

Manet, 1874.
Oil painting. 58¾ × 51½ in. : 149 × 131 cm.

this influence he took to *plein-air* (open-air) painting and an increasingly fresh use of colour, as seen in our plate.

facing the onlooker are so boldly conceived that they could even be separated from the composition. Painted with such verve and with such colouristic virtuosity, this picture has an extraordinarily sharp sense of reality about it. The tones of the woman's dress are found again in the intense blue of the water and the clearer blue of the sky. The white of the man's trousers harmonizes with the sails and the white hull of the boat.

Manet is one of the great painters of women: if his women are not pretty, they are the women we see around us every day, and he conveys to us his own joy and excitement at the idea of presenting them just as they are. His agile brush praises the bloom of radiant flesh, the purity in a turn of the shoulder, the soft firmness of a young breast. A girl in his eyes is nothing less than a bunch of roses, a peony, a branch of lilac . . . Few painters have associated women and flowers as Manet did. We see this in so many of his pictures: a peony thrown at the feet of Eva Gonzales, violets which adorn and perfume his portrait of Berthe Morisot, rhododendrons which bloom behind Madame Guillemet, the little mixed bouquet which he offers here, with good grace, to the 'canotière', the boat-woman of Argenteuil.

In his open-air scenes Manet does not fail to affirm his personal style, so different from that of his friends, the Impressionists. They were pure landscapists, who painted from nature; and the human figure, when it appeared in their work, was merely an accessory. In Manet's pictures, on the contrary, the emphasis is placed entirely on the figures, and the landscape, however carefully painted, is but an accompaniment.

In *Argenteuil*, the couple are painted life size, and the figures and the landscape have been given the intensity of colour which the clarity of the open-air would give them. This is an experiment of great boldness. One thinks of Baudelaire's remark: 'Colourists design like nature: their figures are naturally limited by the harmonious juxtaposition of the coloured masses . . . . they are epic poets . . .'

Jean-Louis Vaudoyer

Bibliography

John Richardson
Manet
Phaidon Press, London, 1958

J-L. Vaudoyer
Manet
Editions du Dimanche, Paris

J-L. Vaudoyer
Les Impressionistes
Les Nouvelles Editions Françaises, Paris, 1948

Clive Bell
French Impressionists
Phaidon Press, London. 1952

Fig. 19b. *Déjeuner sur l'Herbe.*
Edouard Manet, France. 1863.

20A King and Queen

Bronze sculpture by Henry Moore, Shawhead, Dumfries, Gt. Britain. 1952–1953

Plate 20A. *King and Queen. Bronze sculpture by Henry Moore, Gt. Britain. Shawhead, Dumfries, Scotland. 1952–1953. (Size $64\frac{1}{2} \times 54\frac{1}{2} \times 33\frac{1}{4}$ ins.)*

THE *King and Queen* recalls other works of art in this book which portray 'a marriage of association', a quiet, balanced relationship established over a long period of time. Appropriately, there is no suggestion here of passionate emotion, there is no actual physical contact.

The figures are composed, as Moore himself has remarked, of 'a mixture of degrees of realism'. The thin, sensitive arms and the naked feet emphasize the frank humanity of the royal couple. The repetitive curves of their draped bodies give the inert material a sense of life, it suggests the harmony of their relationship, and it invests that relationship with the dignity and calm appropriate to their marriage and their position. Their faces bear little resemblance to human faces and yet they carry with them a convincing reality, an experience clearly understandable in the context of the whole composition – as Moore has explained, 'because a work of art does not aim at reproducing natural appearances, it is not, therefore, an escape from life, but may be penetration into reality.' The head of the king has the quality of a ritual mask, a dramatic image of authority, the force of an individual personality which has enhanced its power by taking upon itself the magic of a ritual object, in this case a crown. The head of the queen, on the other hand, has a soft femininity as it looks out a little vaguely over an imaginary audience. Seated on a hillside, overlooking a Scottish lake, these figures give us one of the most impressive images of the meaning and content of marriage.

Senake Bandaranayake

Henry Moore was born at Castleford, Yorkshire, in 1898. The son of a miner, he first trained as a teacher, fought in the First World War and after the war entered the Leeds School of Art and The Royal College of Art, London. The most influential English sculptor today, he lives at Hadham, near London.

Bibliography

Will Grohmann
The Art of Henry Moore
Thames and Hudson, London, 1960

(Edit.) David Sylvester, Alan Bowness
Henry Moore (3 volumes)
Lund, Humphries and Zwemmer, London, 1957–1965

Geoffrey Grigson
Henry Moore: Heads Figures and Ideas
New York Graphic Society, Greenwich, Connecticut, 1958

20. AMERICAN GOTHIC
Art Institute, Chicago

Grant Wood, 1930.
Oil painting. 29 ⅞ × 25 in. : 75.9 × 63.5 cm.

American Gothic 20

Oil painting by Grant Wood, U.S.A. 1930

Painting in the United States of America begins in the sixteenth century and remains until the twentieth century more or less a provincial manifestation of European art. However, distinctly indigenous traditions emerged from time to time, the most notable of these being the 'primitives' or folk-artists of the eighteenth and nineteenth centuries. These were amateurs and craftsmen such as sign-painters. The earliest of these 'primitives' is John White (1515–1593), an English-born explorer of the sixteenth century, who recorded the life of the American Indians in watercolours of such dramatic simplicity; the most remarkable was the early nineteenth century painter Edward Hicks (1780–1849; see *Man through his Art*, Vol. 1, *War and Peace*, Plate 17). No doubt the work of Grant Wood (born Anamosa, Iowa, 1892; died Iowa City, 1942), directly influenced though it is by his admiration for the Flemish Primitives, owes something to this American tradition. On the other hand, the deeply implanted European tradition in America produced, from the eighteenth century onwards, a considerable body of work which could stand side by side with the best academic work in contemporary Europe. Several American painters settled in Europe and established their reputations there. The Romantic movement of the nineteenth century also produced a number of American landscapists who took their inspiration from their native landscape. Representative of this movement are painters such as Thomas Cole and the so-called 'Hudson River School'. The late nineteenth and twentieth centuries saw the development of an American art which remained bravely independent and was determined to see America through American eyes. One of the earliest and most famous of these painters is Winslow Homer (1836–1910). A subsequent development of this trend, in the twentieth century, was a highly original art which took for its subject the urban landscape of its time. A 'regionalist' version of this trend is represented in some of Grant Wood's best work from which our Plate is taken.

In the last twenty years or so, American painting has taken a dominant role in international art. The work of the American Abstractionists has created everywhere a revolution in styles and techniques, which resembles, in many ways, the revolution created by the

GRANT WOOD MADE HIMSELF KNOWN to the American art world with all the suddenness and shock of an apparition. It happened in 1930, when Wood's *American Gothic* won a bronze medal at a Chicago Art Institute show. It was not the award which mattered, of course, but the extraordinary freshness and bite of the picture itself. The meticulously painted panel combined many old ideas to create a contemporary archetype, the Midwestern farmer, and fix him for all time. As usually happens to close and brilliant observers of character, Wood was first upbraided as unfair, and later – when the truth of his observations began to dawn – hailed as a genius.

He was not a genius and he was never able to repeat his first triumph. But the qualities of inspiration Wood lacked were partly compensated for by a high degree of craftsmanship and sophistication. Technically, *American Gothic* derives from the so-called Flemish primitives, whose paintings of the fifteenth and sixteenth centuries had such astonishing richness of pattern, finish and detail. Wood reflects those qualities in his fascinated attention to such humdrum material as the rickrack braid bordering the woman's apron, the seams of the man's scrupulously clean denim and the roof shingles. But the pose of Wood's couple derives from twentieth-century snapshots. It is head-on, purposefully unimaginative. The man gazes fixedly into the camera eye. The woman's eyes have wandered; she has something on the stove inside. Neither smiles, which is unusual in a snapshot, and this helps to create the vague sense of paradox which gives the picture life. The gothic window, which relates in shape to the woman's hairdo and the man's brows, seems to imply that these people come out from the Middle Ages, yet makes it plain that they are very far indeed from the high-coloured richness of the Gothic world. The pitchfork, thrust abruptly forward like Poseidon's trident, brings to mind how far from salt water these people live.

Wood was thirty-eight when he painted *American Gothic*. He had made a long and painful detour to find his subject matter and his personal method. He was born into a poor farming family in Anamosa, Iowa, and from the time he was ten, when his father died, young Wood had to scratch hard for a living. The boy raised sweet corn and tomatoes to sell from door to door and milked the cows of his more prosperous neighbours. At the lowest point he bought a vacant lot in Cedar Rapids for a dollar down and a dollar a month, built a ten-by-sixteen-foot shack, and lived there with his mother and sister for two years. When times eased, Wood would wander, taking odd jobs and art courses when he found them. The courses led to teaching in public schools, from which he finally saved enough to visit Europe.

In Paris, Wood grew a pinkish beard, parted in the middle. He wore a Basque beret as well, but nothing seemed to help his painting. Concluding at last that all his best ideas 'came while milking a cow', he went home to Iowa, shaved off his whiskers and traded in his beret for a pair of overalls. Then in 1928 the American Legion commissioned him to design a stained-glass window for the Cedar Rapids Memorial Coliseum and staked him to a trip to Munich to learn the necessary techniques. In Munich Wood got his first long look at the Flemish primitives and saw his destiny clear. He came home determined to become the Memling of the Midwest.

'At first', Wood said later, 'I felt I had to search for old things to paint – something soft and mellow. But now I have discovered a decorative quality in American newness.'

Alexander Eliot

*   *   *

The painting of the contemporary American artist Grant Wood is inconceivable without van Eyck's masterpiece (Plate 8). That Grant Wood has given it the title of *American Gothic* is significant. Both works share the stiff, somewhat angular frontality and the emphasis on line as chief elements of composition.

Grant Wood, however, certainly did not intend to create an imitation of a medieval composition. The title itself indicates that he sought to capture the spirit which shaped the people of the New World. For Grant Wood the essence of marriage is not its mystical sacramental character; it is the partnership which has welded together this ageing farmer and his wife in a lifetime of hard work and frugal living. The building behind them does not seem to be a church, but rather a wooden American farm house with its typical porch – and still we do not overlook the gothic window, a faint reminder that Christian tradition has shaped the life and ideals of the puritan settlers.

The Editors

Impressionists in nineteenth century France.

When compared with Henry Moore's *King and Queen* (Plate 20A), Brancusi's *The Kiss* and Zadkine's *The Couple* present completely different aspects of love. In one, the lovers are brought together in one great, sensuous mass, face on face, body to body, arms wrapped around in a thick, protective coil – a dramatic primitive image of physical union ('where each is both'); in the other we have a meeting of emotions, an image of romantic love, delicate, introspective, only just avoiding sentimentality by the careful moulding of one face, the sensitive caricature of the other and the alternately soft and hard geometry of the bodies and hands.

Together these sculptures give us an impression of the variety of twentieth century art, of its re-statement of perpetual themes.

Bibliography

Alexander Eliot
American Painting
Time Inc., New York, 1957

Fig. 20a. *The Kiss. Constantin Brancusi. 1908.*

Fig. 20b. *The Couple. Ossip Zadkine. 1931.*